Before Victoria

EXTRAORDINARY WOMEN *of* the BRITISH ROMANTIC ERA

Before Victoria

EXTRAORDINARY WOMEN *of*
the BRITISH ROMANTIC ERA

by ELIZABETH CAMPBELL DENLINGER
Foreword by LYNDALL GORDON

The New York Public Library/Columbia University Press

New York

2005

Published on the occasion of the exhibition
Before Victoria: Extraordinary Women of the British Romantic Era
presented at The New York Public Library
Humanities and Social Sciences Library
D. Samuel and Jeane H. Gottesman Exhibition Hall
April 8–July 30, 2005

This publication and the exhibition were made possible in part by The Carl and Lily Pforzheimer Foundation, Inc., and The New York Public Library's Carl H. Pforzheimer Collection of Shelley and His Circle.

Additional support for this publication was provided by Sue and Edgar Wachenheim III and by the Bertha and Isaac Liberman Foundation, Inc., in memory of Ruth and Seymour Klein.

Support for The New York Public Library's Exhibitions Program has been provided by Pinewood Foundation and by Sue and Edgar Wachenheim III.

Illustrations are drawn from the following collections of The New York Public Library's Humanities and Social Sciences Library: the Carl H. Pforzheimer Collection of Shelley and His Circle; the Miriam and Ira D. Wallach Division of Art, Prints and Photographs, Print Collection; the Henry W. and Albert A. Berg Collection of English and American Literature; the General Research Division; the Rare Books Division; and the Spencer Collection.

Karen Van Westering
Manager, NYPL Publications
Anne Skillion *Senior Editor*
Barbara Bergeron *Editor*
Jennifer Woolf *Photography Coordinator*

Designed by Kara Van Woerden

www.nypl.org

Copyright © 2005 by The New York Public Library, Astor, Lenox and Tilden Foundations

Foreword copyright © 2005 by Lyndall Gordon

Photograph on page 166 ©Peter Aaron/Esto

The name "The New York Public Library" and the lion logo are registered marks and the property of The New York Public Library, Astor, Lenox and Tilden Foundations.

Columbia University Press books are printed on permanent and durable acid-free paper.
Printed in China
c 10 9 8 7 6 5 4 3 2 1
p 10 9 8 7 6 5 4 3 2 1

Library of Congress Cataloging-in-Publication Data

Denlinger, Elizabeth Campbell.
 Before Victoria : extraordinary women of the British Romantic era / by Elizabeth Campbell Denlinger.
   p. cm.
 "Published on the occasion of the exhibition, Before Victoria: extraordinary women of the British Romantic era, presented at the New York Public Library, Humanities and Social Sciences Library, D. Samuel and Jeane H. Gottesman Exhibition Hall, April 8–July 30, 2005"—T.p. verso.
 Includes bibliographical references (p.) and index.
 ISBN 0-231-13630-7 (Columbia University Press : alk. paper) — ISBN 0-231-13631-5 (Columbia University Press : pbk. : alk. paper)
 1. Women—Great Britain—Biography. 2. Great Britain—History—1789–1820—Biography. 3. Great Britain—History—1800–1837—Biography. 4. Great Britain—Social conditions—18th century. 5. Great Britain—Social conditions—19th century. 6. Great Britain—Biography. I. New York Public Library. II. Title.
 CT3320.D46 2005
 305.4′0941′09034–DC22

                                   2004059267

Columbia University Press
Publishers Since 1893
New York Chichester, West Sussex

www.columbia.edu/cu/cup

CONTENTS

FOREWORD
Lyndall Gordon

Who were the women in the late eighteen hundreds and early nineteen hundreds who set themselves apart from social expectations? *Before Victoria*, drawing primarily on The New York Public Library's great Pforzheimer Collection,[1] opens up the lives of an array of women who turned away from the beaten track during the fifty years before the rise of "the Woman Question," the more familiar movement that took off during Victoria's reign.

In 1787, two years before the French Revolution, Mary Wollstonecraft was a restless governess, reading Rousseau in an Irish castle and collecting matter for her first novel, *Mary* (1788). "The soul of the author" was to animate "the hidden springs" of a new kind of being called by her own name: "in a fiction, such a being may be allowed to exist; ... not subjugated to opinion; but drawn by the individual from the original source."

Later that year she took the novel to London, determined to shed the limited occupations open to women. She meant to find a new plot of existence for her sex. "I am ... going to be the first of a new genus," she confided to her sister Everina. "I am not born to tread in the beaten track – the peculiar bent of my nature pushes me on." When "Mary" in the novel rejects the practice of "giving" a bride in marriage, the author herself was germinating the new character who found fruition in *A Vindication of the Rights of Woman* (1792). Every phase of her life was an experiment: the school she set up in her twenties, her years in France during the Terror, her travels to Scandinavia, and her unconventional union with William Godwin, the foremost radical philosopher of the day. As we trace her experiments, above all "that most fruitful experiment," her relation with Godwin, we see everywhere a single purpose: to center the affections as a counter to the twin predators of violence and commerce.

Her one-time pupil Margaret King Moore, Lady Mount Cashell also broke with women's traditions. In 1806 she abandoned her aristocratic life and disguised herself as a man in order to attend medical lectures at the University of Jena. She went on to practice medicine in Pisa (in the respectable guise of helping the poor), rejecting harsh and hopeless interventions as well as lucrative drugs, in favor of gentler cures, particularly with children, and better use of the body's own curative powers. Mary Shelley, Wollstonecraft's daughter, earned her living as a writer, most famously as author of *Frankenstein*. Her stepsister, Claire Clairmont, played the overture to Rossini's new opera *Cenerentola*, and her voice, trained to performer's standard, thrilled their Pisa circle in one of Shelley's greatest poems, "To Constantia, Singing." After Shelley's death, Clairmont supported herself as a governess in what she called "my ice cave" – Russia – where she developed

Wollstonecraft's innovative ideas of education, and wrote letters yet to be recognized as among the best in the English language. The achievements of this generation were all the braver in the context of counterrevolution, its silencing of women and their obligatory retreat from the public arena.

There were others, like the novelist Mary Hays, who tried out the character Wollstonecraft had brought into being. The future poet Elizabeth Barrett was only twelve in 1818 when she read the *Rights of Woman*. At fourteen she would declare her "natural" independence of mind and "spurn" the triviality of women's lives. Similarly, in 1825, a daughter of a New England clergyman published her thoughts on "The Natural Rights of Woman." The Creator, she argues, crowned his labors by giving being to the most intelligent of his creatures:

Male and female created he them; but declared them of "one bone – one flesh" – one mind. *To* them *he directed his divine commands – and gave them rule over all he had made....*

But it seems that man *soon became wiser than his Maker, and discovered that the Almighty was mistaken ... and that all the mind ... had been bestowed on* himself, *and that* woman *had received only ... the mere leavings, and scrapings that could be gathered after his own wise brain was furnished.*

Twelve years before the founding of Mount Holyoke, the first women's college, the author is hopeful of the schoolhouse with its custom of equal education, and fewer inducements to phoniness. To be sure, girls still leave with nothing more than "a smattering of *terms*," but "we feel the influence of the female character" in some shift from modish sensibility toward "sympathy for real distress."

Curiously, this author's name was Mary Wollstonecraft. It was not an invention or coincidence. This American Wollstonecraft, a botanist, was in fact the widow of an English immigrant, Charles, youngest brother of the more famous Mary.

In Britain's Cape Colony in the late 1870s, Olive Schreiner, a young governess in a lean-to room on a rocky stretch of veld, wrote a novel about a New Woman. Though she appears an oddity on a backward, colonial farm, she does not yield her conviction of who she is in order to pursue the mediocre plots open to her sex. An authentic self seems to speak out of a stark and timeless landscape. When Schreiner brought her novel to London, her eloquence broke in on the earnest deliberations of the Men and Women's Club for redefining the nature of the sexes. Her manner was visionary, her gestures emphatic, her dark eyes glowed as she looked back to the author of *A Vindication of the Rights of Woman*. Mary Wollstonecraft, she says, is "one of ourselves." Nearly a century earlier this woman had foreseen "the mighty sexual change that is coming upon us." In the

1880s the two sexes seemed still a mystery, "what in their inmost nature they are…. Future ages will have to solve it."

The nineteenth century pressed the issue of the vote and education; the twentieth century, that of professional advancement; but the subtler issue of our nature is still to be resolved. In 1869 John Stuart Mill, the first to propose women's suffrage in the British Parliament, says, "what is now called the nature of women is an eminently artificial thing." In 1915 Virginia Woolf predicts that it will take six generations for women to come into their own – if so, we're not there yet. "The great problem is the true nature of woman," she alerts students at Cambridge. If this century is to solve it, the gender revolution in the late eighteenth century and its heirs in the next generation offer a start.

In the period covered by the present volume, a new-found creature – "almost unclassified" – was crawling out from under the stone of history. In the early 1830s a Yorkshire schoolgirl called Ellen Nussey, visiting Haworth Parsonage, witnessed the young Brontë sisters marching round the dining-room table – as she relates in her manuscript recollections in the Library's Berg Collection. At nine o'clock, when their aunt retired, the three sisters put away their sewing, blew out the candles, and began to pace the room, their forms glancing into the firelight, then out into the shadow. Ellen thought they blew out the candles for economy, but darkness freed them to be what they were. When, later, Charlotte Brontë's Lucy Snowe is asked "who are you," she replies, "I am a rising character."

A past experience revived for its meaning, T. S. Eliot said, is "not the experience of one life only / But of many generations." Women of the present generation, in the choices and opportunities open to us, are heirs of the "new genus" that came to life among the deviant throngs of artists, mistresses, bluestockings, gamblers, and criminals during the fifty years before Victoria.

Goddess in tattered petticoats

Wealthy aristocratic women had more freedom than other women if they dared to take it. James Gillray's Diana Return'd from the Chace *(1802) shows Mary Amelia Cecil, Countess of Salisbury (1750–1835), as a modern Diana (the goddess of the hunt), jubilant as she holds the fox's tail aloft. Gillray is satirizing women who hunted, but his subject also conveys a winning and exuberant energy.* PRINT COLLECTION

PREFACE

Before Victoria aims to show how a group of unusual women contributed to British culture at a historical moment that was, as they might have said, big with change – pregnant, that is, with years in which the lives of Britons were nearly transformed. Its temporal scope is the Romantic era in the historical sense of the term, covering the decades between 1789, when the French Revolution began, and 1837, when Victoria acceded to the throne of the United Kingdom. This has been, recently, a contested era: some historians argue that the years just before Victoria saw women increasingly confined to the private sphere, and less able to speak their minds if they did venture into public. Others contend that while codes of behavior became more restrictive on men and women, and more stratified by class, women nonetheless accomplished a great deal in these years. *Before Victoria*, inevitably, comes down on the second side, since its focus is on women who, for better or worse, put themselves out of the ordinary course of life. Its task will have been accomplished if the reader is left with an appreciation for both the multiple restrictions – social, legal, sexual, and economic – on women's lives in these years, and for how much women were able to accomplish in spite of them.

The book itself may be thought of, in a wide sense, as a portrait gallery. The chapters present sketches in biography, bringing together women from very different areas of life: wives, mothers, and lovers are here, but so are actresses, botanists, poets, novelists, travelers, sculptors, astronomers, courtesans, and utopians. They also present a wide variety of images: portraits in oils, satirical cartoons, caricatures, squibs, watercolors, and photographs – drawn from the collections of The New York Public Library, and above all from the Carl H. Pforzheimer Collection of Shelley and His Circle. (For a brief history of the collection, see Stephen Wagner's Afterword.)

These images, and others, were part of an exhibition presented in 2005 at the Library, to which this book is the companion volume. The Pforzheimer is one of the premier collections in British Romanticism in the United States, and selecting texts and images from its holdings meant choosing from an embarrassment of riches. Hardly less important has been the Library's Miriam and Ira D. Wallach Division of Art, Prints and Photographs, from which some of the most striking and beautiful images were selected.

This book was not written primarily for scholars, but for readers whose imaginations have been piqued by reading, say, *Frankenstein*, or *Pride and Prejudice*, or Ann Radcliffe's *Mysteries of Udolpho*, who want to gain a wider sense of what life was like for women in Britain soon before the first era that feels to us "modern" – which is to say, the Victorian – began. In the 1780s the night was lit only by candles and lanterns; land travel required horses or sturdy shoes, and water travel required sails. The only records of human faces were made by paint or pencil. It was illegal to be a landowning Catholic, Jews were not citizens, and Africans were enslaved in Britain and its expanding empire. Married women disappeared legally under their husbands' identities and had no rights to children or property. By the early years of Victoria's reign, the streets of London, at least, were largely gas-lit, and to someone used to electric lighting would not have looked unfamiliar. Railways were the normal mode of land travel, and steamships had become a common sight in inland waters. There were many more shops, and more goods to buy in them, displayed in plate-glass windows. Catholic emancipation had gone through in 1829; slavery, even in the British colonies, had been made illegal in 1833. Jews were not granted British citizenship until 1858, and married women still did not have rights to their children or property. However, they might, like other people living in these years, be photographed, and they might have chloroform to ease the pains of childbirth.

Mary Wollstonecraft, the pioneering writer on women's lives and women's rights, pressed for changes that went beyond what the Victorians would be able to make. She was keenly aware of the difficulties of her time, writing of her eldest daughter, still an infant: "I feel more than a mother's fondness and anxiety, when I reflect on the dependent and oppressed state of her sex. I dread lest she should be forced to sacrifice her heart to her principles, or principles to her heart."[1] Some of the women whose lives are described in *Before Victoria* did make one or the other of these sacrifices; some refused to do so. The most significant aspect of the gallery is its variety: some women are extraordinary because they refused to abide by the conventions of their time, others because they embody them to a surpassing degree. All of the women here were conscious, on some level, of the "dependent and oppressed state" of their sex; but self-pity takes one only so far, and in the next paragraph Wollstonecraft picks herself up, with "[W]ither am I wandering?" The women of *Before Victoria* found as many different answers to this question as they had lives.

Chapter One

MARY ROBINSON,
EIGHTEENTH-CENTURY ROMANTIC

THE LIFE OF MARY DARBY ROBINSON, actress, mistress, poet, mother, and novelist, illustrates the state of England and of Englishwomen during the shift from the eighteenth century to the Romantic era. Born in 1757 and dying, aged only forty-three, as the eighteenth century ended and the nineteenth began, Robinson is at once exemplary and extraordinary: exemplary because she embodied so many of the possibilities open to women, and extraordinary because she lived out these possibilities for her own reasons and by her own lights.[1] Her early life was conducted according to eighteenth-century possibilities and expectations: beginning as a virtuous wife, she became an actress famous for her beauty, and, in the best tradition of royal courtesans, had an affair with the Prince of Wales. She soon discovered that she had placed herself outside respectable English society: a woman's sexual reputation, once stained, was treated like a signboard on which any sort of rumor might be posted, and London gossips provided plenty of material without too much reference to its validity.

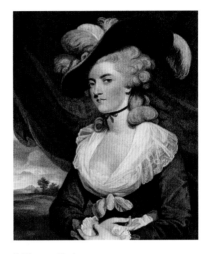

A Romantic icon
Mary Robinson, by Sir Joshua Reynolds. The poet Samuel Taylor Coleridge said of her:
"I never knew a human being with so full a mind – bad, good, and indifferent, I grant you, but full and overflowing." Engraving by W. Dickinson, 1785. PRINT COLLECTION

While ordinary women who were rumored to be having sex outside wedlock had only their neighbors to worry about, Robinson found herself caricatured by James Gillray and Thomas Rowlandson, whose satirical cartoons inform our view of the period. But Robinson also had unusual advantages: flattering images, engraved after paintings by Gainsborough, Romney, and Reynolds, among others, were recognized by thousands of people who never saw her in the flesh. The advent of these mass-produced images signals the transition from the older "face-to-face" culture, in which one's world was composed of people one knew, to one in which newspapers and magazines made glamorous strangers familiar. The first part of Robinson's life, during which her picture circulated around Britain as she and her carriage did around London – for she enjoyed her years of fame – illustrates this transition.

After 1783, Robinson's life became less public when she suffered partial paralysis, possibly from a miscarriage. In later years she kept herself before the public eye in a different way: in addition to allowing her image to be spread everywhere, she disseminated her own words and published extensively. By the last year of her life, Mary Robinson had remade herself into both a Romantic heroine and a Romantic poet. What did this mean? Practically, it meant that she edited the poetry section of a newspaper and exchanged verses with a young poet named Samuel Taylor Coleridge; she admired *Lyrical Ballads*, which he and William Wordsworth published in 1798, now seen as a landmark of Romantic poetry. Quite independently of Wordsworth and Coleridge, she had published a volume of her own called *Lyrical Tales*. Artistically, it meant that the poetry Robinson was writing in 1800 would ally her with other Romantic poets.

In the traditional understanding of the term, Romantic artists prize the emotional over the rational, finding heroes and heroines in madmen and madwomen and, generally, in the members of the social body who suffer most. They value nature, solitude, and the sublime over cities, company, and mere prettiness. They tend toward mysticism in religion, and liberalism in politics. One of the most famous moments of British Romantic poetry is Wordsworth's recollection of his visit to France soon after the Revolution: "Bliss was it in that dawn to be alive, / But to be young was very Heaven!"[2] Romantic artists believe that private integrity is more important than public reputation, that human beings are naturally good and that evil is a perversion of human character. Above all, Romantic artists see art as a vocation, where the eighteenth century often saw it as a profession or a craft. By the time of her death, Robinson was crippled, impoverished, dying, and nearly forgotten by the public. She wrote ceaselessly from a cottage in Windsor Forest on the outskirts of London with only her beloved daughter for company, and between writing and suffering she was an inspiration to both Coleridge and to herself. In this position, she was exactly the kind of disenfranchised, isolated, pained character on whom Romantic poets loved to dwell.

The world into which Mary Robinson was born in 1757 was local, intimate, bawdy, often corrupt, sometimes frolicsome, its inhabitants divided into many small groups based on blood, trade, religion, custom, and geography. Although Britons were conscious of and anxious about hierarchy and social distinctions, these were no longer as rigid as they had been in the early 1700s. By 1837, when the sixteen-year-old Victoria took the throne, the population of England and Wales (not including Ireland) had risen to about 15.9 million, from about 6.2 million a century before.[3] Face-to-face culture had been replaced with one defined by print: a nation of neighbors had been replaced by one of novel readers. The small groups into which the population had been divided were melded to a perceptible degree into larger social classes: these included the aristocracy and gentry, but also growing numbers of industrial laborers, domestic servants, and a group that in the late eighteenth century began to be called "the middle class."[4]

Robinson's family belonged to the mercantile part of this last group. Her father, Nicholas Darby, was a sea captain in Bristol, then the second largest city in England and a center of the slave trade. She was taught at a school run by the Misses More, five sisters who taught the basics for girls – reading, writing, arithmetic, sewing – as well as the accomplishments: dancing, singing, French, Italian. Hannah More, the next-to-youngest of the sisters, would become one of Britain's most prominent exponents of evangelical Christianity and conservative thought. In the 1760s, however, she was simply a young teacher, and in that capacity accompanied Mary Darby and other girls from the school to the opening night of the just-built theater in Bristol. Both the girl and the young woman were stage-struck, along with many others; the eighteenth century was one of the great periods of British theater, and the successful opening of theaters in smaller cities like Bristol was part of the growing urbanization and sophistication of British culture.

Mary Darby was still too young to do more than dream (if indeed she did) of going on the stage. During these years, the learning she obtained saved her – as education saved many other girls like her – from a future of real poverty. Boarding school education was not deep, but it left girls with imagination and energy, ready to earn a living by their pens. In any case, her family's fortunes soon took a turn for the worse: her father embarked on a fishing venture in Labrador, and took up with another woman. Her mother, Hester, moved the family to London – then, as it had been for centuries, by far the largest city in Britain and a magnet for all who wished to make a new start. She availed herself there of one of the few respectable means by which a genteel woman could earn a living, and set up a school of her own. On the failure of his Canadian venture, Nicholas Darby returned to England and forced her to close it, fearing that a working wife would damage his reputation. This was entirely legal, and Hester Darby was without recourse. Years later, when Mary Robinson's friend Mary Wollstonecraft wrote a political treatise in vindication of the rights of woman, and a novel in protest of the wrongs against them, this was the sort of injustice she had in mind.

It was perhaps these difficulties that led Mary Darby to marry so young, the faster to take herself off her mother's hands. She did, at any rate, marry a young law clerk named Thomas Robinson before she was eighteen, only to discover that he had considerably misrepresented his income. Worse, he gambled, and soon betrayed her with other women. According to her posthumously published *Memoirs*, when he was imprisoned for debt she went with him, as a good wife did, into the Fleet Prison, where he conducted his intrigues even within the prison walls.

In prison Robinson helped her husband by a time-honored tactic: she found a patron, Georgiana Spencer Cavendish, the Duchess of Devonshire. They met in a way that was conceivable only in the intimate world mentioned above.

A talent for self-transformation

Mary Robinson's glamour and talent for self-transformation made her a much-watched figure in her time. The object of gossip and satire as the Prince of Wales's mistress, and an extraordinary beauty painted by the best portraitists, Robinson herself adopted the persona of Sappho, famous as a woman poet who suffered for love. To make a living, she wrote novels such as Vancenza.

1 *The posthumous chapbook version of Mary Robinson's* Vancenza *(London, 1810).* PFORZHEIMER COLLECTION

2 *Mary Robinson. Engraving by George Smith, after George Romney, 1781.* PRINT COLLECTION

3 *Frontispiece from Mary Robinson,* Sappho and Phaon *(London, 1796).* PFORZHEIMER COLLECTION

4 *A satirical rendering of Mary Robinson and the Prince of Wales in facing cameos, from* Town and Country Magazine *(London, January 1781).* GENERAL RESEARCH DIVISION

1

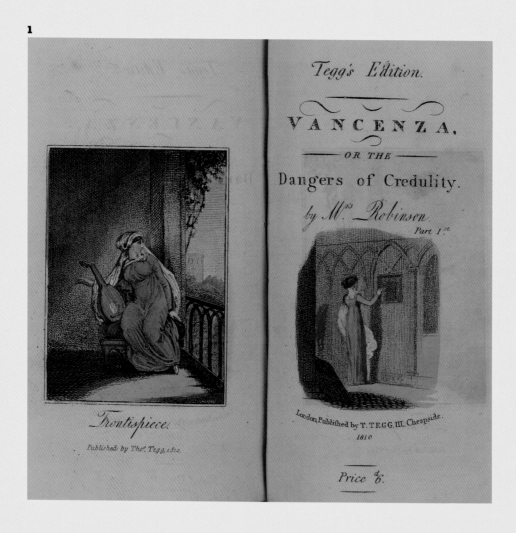

Frontispiece.

Published by Thos. Tegg, 1810.

Tegg's Edition.

VANCENZA,

— OR THE —

Dangers of Credulity.

by Mrs. Robinson.

Part 1st

London, Published by T. TEGG, III. Cheapside.
1810

Price 6d.

2

3

S A P P H O.

Engraved for M.ʳˢ *Robinson's Sonnets,
from a Marble Bust in the Palace
of the Prince Giustiniani at Rome.*

Nᵒ II.   Nᵒ III.

The fair Ophelia.   *The illustrious Heir.*

Published by A. Hamilton Juⁿ. Fleet Street Feb.ʸ 1, 1781.

4

Robinson sent her recently published *Poems* (1775) to the Duchess, using her brother, "a charming youth," as messenger – simply on the strength of having heard that the Duchess was fond of poetry. These were apprentice works on hackneyed late eighteenth-century models, but the Duchess was not a literary critic, and her generous response was an invitation to visit. (Robinson, since she was not the debtor herself, could enter and leave the Fleet at will.) The two young women liked each other, and the Duchess of Devonshire, an extraordinarily kind woman, offered friendship and some limited pecuniary aid.

Thus far, Robinson had lived a completely eighteenth-century life. Patronage of the sort she received from the Duchess, indeed, continued a tradition that goes back much further than the eighteenth century. Robinson's next steps, too, were so typical of the period that they are better described as stereotypical: penniless and adorable, with a toddler daughter and an unfaithful husband, she went on the stage at Richard Brinsley Sheridan's Drury Lane Theatre. She became a moderately successful actress, celebrated as much for her beauty as her talent, known for playing "breeches roles" that called for women to dress as men; in an era of gowns that reached the ground, this was a titillating way to show a woman's legs. The Prince of Wales – the future George IV, who would be Regent from 1811 to 1820 – saw her perform as Perdita in Shakespeare's *Winter's Tale* and fell in love with her – thus, at least, Robinson's memoirs have it; there is evidence that in fact they had met before this.[5] After a good deal of anonymous wooing by messenger, he won her as his mistress. He would sign his notes "Florizel," after the prince in the play. The affair lasted less than two years, but it was to haunt Robinson for the rest of her life. She was known by the name Perdita – "the lost one" – ever after. Indeed, if one of the requirements for being a Romantic female character is a certain degree of pathos (and there is every sign that Robinson cast herself in this role), she could not have chosen a better Shakespearean source than this bittersweet comedy.

Life, however, does not work according to plot devices, and although Robinson's *Memoirs* don't say so, she seems to have quite enjoyed her liaison with the prince. Certainly she enjoyed the publicity, riding in a carriage emblazoned with a basket that suspiciously resembled a coronet, and changing her appearance constantly: "To-day she was a *paysanne*, with her straw hat tied at the back of her head.... Yesterday she perhaps had been the dressed belle of Hyde Park, trimmed, powdered, patched, painted to the utmost power of rouge and white lead. Tomorrow she would be the cravatted Amazon of the riding-house; but be she what she might, hats of the fashionable promenaders swept the ground as she passed."[6]

After the liaison with the Prince of Wales ended, there were, apparently, other men – the liberal politician Charles James Fox, the Earl of Cholmondeley, the Duke of Dorset, among others. It is not possible to say whether or not these rumors were true. More important is the fact that Robinson, over the next few years, gained the reputation of a courtesan, a woman famous for what she wore, where she went, and whom she slept with. In the mid-1780s courtesans had a transitional social status: already unmentionable in respectable company, such women's names were on their way to being unprintable in the respectable press; but in these years everyone still liked to read about them. It was the beginning of a celebrity culture as we know it now, and many of the instruments of that culture – newspapers, magazines, gossip columns, cheaply reproducible images – were already available. Mary Robinson appeared in all of them, although the paradoxical consequence of her status as the prince's mistress was that her theatrical career was largely curtailed.[7]

Robinson's very visible life and the theatricality of her constant costume-changes became less acceptable over the 1780s and 90s, and one of the differences between the eighteenth century and the Romantic period is that the proper sphere for women seemed, ever more clearly, the domestic one: "[F]or a woman – 'the post of honor is a private station,'" as the poet Charlotte Smith wrote.[8] Other poets, Felicia Hemans in particular, asserted that women were rooted to family and home as men were not. Women were able to learn very clearly what was expected of them from conduct books that were both popular reading and popular gifts, especially, one suspects, from parents who wished their teenaged daughters to learn how to behave better than their fashionable boarding schools had taught them.

Yet this emphasis on privacy and domesticity should not be understood as a sentence passed on all women, forbidding them to stir outside without a chaperone. Nor, of course, was the encouragement to domesticity new in the late eighteenth century. Women might be given conduct books, and they might even buy them for their own edification, but we should not assume that they followed their directions on how to conduct themselves any more than readers now follow diet books to the letter. Nonetheless, as the general ideas of diet books today float about the conversational atmosphere, so, to some degree, did the ideas of conduct books in the later eighteenth century and well into the nineteenth. Some women must have taken them quite seriously; some must have looked at the advice they were offered and laughed. Lives like Mary Robinson's show us that some women reacted to a more forbidding public atmosphere by insisting on their right to move about freely. And while Robinson attracted her share of hostile publicity, she was also much admired.

Even so, the shift in ideology did mean that a different style of movement became necessary for women, inwardly more conscious of the demands of propriety and outwardly more conscious of the eyes of the neighbors and servants. There were plenty of women who had liaisons with men outside of wedlock during the nineteenth century, and even a few women who insisted that love and not

Guides for living

Conduct books offered advice on manners, religion, education, courtship, and love. Heavy on morality and short on fun, they were given by parents and schools to girls entering the marriage market (who likely preferred The Science of Love *to* Letters on the Improvement of the Mind*). Mrs. Beeton's extremely popular guide to good housekeeping was a later, more secular development.*

1

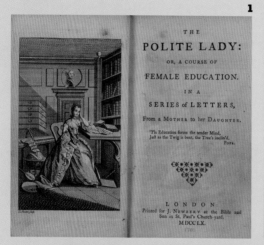

3

4

5

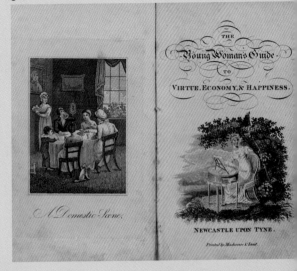

6

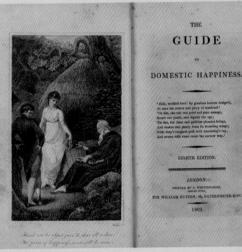

7

1 *Charles Allen*, The Polite Lady: or, A Course of Female Education. In a Series of Letters, from a Mother to Her Daughter *(London, 1760)*.

2 *Sarah Pennington*, An Unfortunate Mother's Advice to Her Absent Daughters *(London, 1803)*.

3 The Science of Love, or, The Whole Art of Courtship, Made Familiar to Every Capacity, Containing Love-letters, Pleasing Conversations, Poems, & Songs. To Which Is Added an Appendix Instructing Persons of Both Sexes in the Choice of a Companion for Life *(London, 1792)*.

4 *Mrs. Hester Chapone*, Letters on the Improvement of the Mind: Addressed to a Lady *(London, 1808)*.

5 *John Armstrong*, The Young Woman's Guide to Virtue, Economy, and Happiness *(Newcastle upon Tyne, ca. 1825)*.

6 *Mrs. Isabella Beeton*, The Book of Household Management *(London, 1861)*.

7 *William Giles*, The Guide to Domestic Happiness *(London, 1809)*.

vows made the important bond – the novelist George Eliot, for instance, who lived in an unmarried union with her fellow-writer George Henry Lewes. But the gaiety of Robinson's early career, and her pleasure in making a public spectacle of herself, would have been impossible in the nineteenth century.

In the mid-1780s, Robinson began a long-term relationship with Banastre Tarleton, a hero of the American Revolutionary War. They would never marry, since she was still the wife of Thomas Robinson. Divorce allowing remarriage was possible only through a private act of Parliament, and even a legal separation was difficult, expensive, and embarrassing to obtain. And, then, Robinson's reputation was deeply stained; eventually Tarleton would leave her to marry and have children with a young woman from a suitable family.

In these years, however, he had recently left the army and was the Whig Member of Parliament for the growing city of Liverpool, on the mid-west coast of England. He was not known in civilian life for his intelligence, and Robinson gave him considerable help strategizing election campaigns and writing speeches.[9] His positions, on the whole, were liberal, as Mary Robinson's were. She believed that the vote should be extended to more than the tiny number of Britons (all men, and mostly landowners) who held it; she believed that birth and inheritance were far too powerful, and that room needed to be made for talented men and women without money or title; she believed that the rich had a responsibility to their nation that was ill repaid by their constant gambling; and she believed, along with many other Britons, both Whig and Tory, that the slave trade was wicked.

Whatever Banastre Tarleton believed privately, however, anti-slavery was hardly a position he could hold in public: his constituents, the merchants of Liverpool, made most of their money from buying people in Africa and selling them to plantations in the West Indies, or trading them for the sugar produced there by slave labor. Ironically, Robinson's support for her lover may have extended to writing Tarleton's parliamentary speeches defending what she privately thought was indefensible. Robinson's own writing was firmly abolitionist, and her love for Tarleton may have led her into a deeply self-contradictory position. It was on such positions, as much as those supporting outright conquest, that the British empire was built.

Robinson's better self, however, believed in liberty, equality, and fraternity, and when the French Revolution began in 1789, she wrote a long poem, "Ainsi va le monde" ("So goes the world") to celebrate its promise. 1789 is one of the traditional dates by which to mark the beginning of the Romantic movement, and certainly, at least in Europe, the Revolution was the most important event of the century. It signified, suddenly and unmistakably, that things might be very different, that life might be arranged more equitably, that the unimportant people of the world might not always be the ones who paid for the pleasures of the rich. Robinson had a good deal of company, for many Britons reacted with joy at the

Mary Robinson on display

Mary Robinson appears here (at right; see detail on page 2) as Londoners often saw her, surrounded by a crowd of admirers at Vauxhall Gardens, one of the new pleasure parks designed for nighttime use. Visitors could range about the refreshment stands, box seats, tree-lined pathways, and ring for promenading, while watching concerts, fireworks displays, and, above all, other members of the fashionable world. Vaux-Hall, engraving by R. Pollard, after Thomas Rowlandson, 1784. PRINT COLLECTION

NEW MORALITY;— or —The promis'd Installment of the High-Priest of the

"————behold!——————
"The Directorial LAMA, Sovereign Priest
"LEPAUX —whom Atheists worship —at whose nod
"Bow their meek heads — the Men without a God!
"——Ere long, perhaps, to this astonish'd Isle
Fresh from the Shores of subjugated Nile,
Shall BUONAPARTE'S victor Fleet protect
The genuine Theo-philanthropic Sect—

The Sect of MARAT, MIRABEAU, VOLTAIRE,
Led by their Pontiff, good LA-REVEILLERE.
Rejoicd our CLUBS shall greet him, and Install
The holy Hunch-back in thy Dome, St. PAUL,
While countless votaries thronging in his train
Wave their Red Caps, and hymn this jocund strain:
"Couriers and Stars, Seditions Evening Host,
"Thou Morning Chronicle, and Morning Post,

"Whether ye make the Rights of
"Your Country libel, and yo
"Or dirt on private worth an
"Still blasphemous and black
"——And ye five other wanderi
"In sweet accord of harmony
"C———DGE and S——TH—Y, L—
"Tune all your mystic harps

...LANTHROPES, with the Homage of Leviathan and his Suite.—

"PR_TL_Y and W_F_LD, humble, holy men,
"Give praises to his name with tongue and pen!—
"TH_LW_L, and ye that Lecture as ye go,
"And for your pains get Pelted, praise LE PAUX!—
"Praise him each Jacobin, or Fool, or Knave,
"And your cropp'd heads in sign of worship wave!—
"All creeping creatures, venomous and low,
"PAINE, W_LL_MS, G_DW_N, H_LC_FT, praise LEPAUX!—

"And thou LEVIATHAN! on Ocean's brim
"Hugest of living things that sleep & swim;
"Thou in whose nose by BURKE'S gigantic hand
"The hook was fixed to drag thee to the land
"With ___, ___, and ___ in thy train,
"And W_____ wallowing in the Yeasty main,
"Still as ye snort, and puff, and spout, and blow;
"In puffing, and in spouting, praise LEPAUX!—_Vide. Anti-Jacobin_

Published. August 1st 1798. by J. Wright N.169. Piccadilly. for the Anti-Jacobin Magazine & Review—

J.s Gillray, invt & fect

Reactions to the French Revolution

The caricaturist James Gillray began by satirizing everyone – Whigs and Tories, radical atheists as well as evangelical Christians – but the Tory government purchased his services with a secret pension, paid to him from late 1797 until early 1801 (when the Tories lost power). Here, in an illustration from The Anti-Jacobin Magazine and Review, _he savages literary supporters of the French Revolution: Mary Robinson's novels pour out of the "cornucopia of ignorance," while the poets Coleridge and Robert Southey, shown as asses, kneel to receive its bounty. James Gillray,_ New Morality; – or The Promis'd Installment of the High-Priest of the Theophilanthropes, _1798._ PFORZHEIMER COLLECTION

TO HENRY HUNT, ESQ⁼

Early struggle for the vote

At least eleven people were killed, and hundreds wounded, when the local militia galloped into a peaceful crowd gathered at St. Peter's Field outside Manchester on August 16, 1819. Their demand was political reform, starting with the vote, which was then highly restricted. The attack – quickly dubbed the "Peterloo Massacre," after the French loss at Waterloo – shocked Britons everywhere, and the injuries inflicted on women, who had worn white to show the purity of their cause, drew particular outrage. An anonymous artist titled this contemporaneous etching and aquatint To Henry Hunt, Esq., one of the speakers at the meeting.

PFORZHEIMER COLLECTION

early news of the Revolution. It seemed briefly that France was on its way to a parliamentary monarchy like their own, in which power was balanced between the king and the two Houses of Parliament. The changes in French law, besides extending the right to vote – though not so far as giving women suffrage – included a liberalization of divorce laws, a loosening of parents' control over their children, and abolition of the aristocracy.

When fundamental change begins in one place, it gives hope to those elsewhere, and considerable numbers of workers and artisans in Britain felt that revolution did not need to stop with France. Groups such as the London Corresponding Society held mass meetings to support political reform, making demands that now seem self-evident: the right to vote, which they demanded for all adult men, was the first of these. It is difficult now to imagine a world in which the word "democracy" carried as much power to shock as it did in 1789, but the word's root sense, "the rule of the people," was entirely antithetical to a government arranged by and for the rich and well-born. As happens with any revolution, people of all classes could not stop talking and arguing about the meaning, extent, and implications of the events in France. Publications vindicating the rights of men, then women, then (satirically) children and animals were published. Robinson read and was heartened by two works of her friend Mary Wollstonecraft: the *Vindication of the Rights of Men* (1790), a response to the conservative politician Edmund Burke, and the more surprising *Vindication of the Rights of Woman* (1792). While Mary Robinson did not write a political work until later in life, the novels she had begun to write in 1791 – largely to bring in money – are full of characters gleefully arguing about the Revolution, with those in favor awarded all the best lines.

But this early hopeful phase did not last long, and Edmund Burke's pessimistic view of the Revolution came, after 1792, to be the one that most Britons shared. In particular the days of the 1793 Terror, when Maximilien Robespierre kept the blades of the guillotines wet with blood, turned the stomachs and changed the minds of many former supporters of the Revolution. Robinson herself had, in earlier days, been the guest of Marie Antoinette in Paris, and wrote a monody to the memory of the French queen, who followed her husband to the guillotine in 1793. At home, the government of England cracked down harshly on all resistance and paid for propaganda in prints like James Gillray's 1798 *New Morality* (see pages 14–15). The war against the intellectuals is the focus here, and Robinson's novel *Walsingham* is portrayed as part of the new rubbish to come from the supporters of the Revolution, along with other print and human icons of what was derisively known as English Jacobinism.

By 1800, the year of Robinson's death, Britain had been at war with France and her allies for eight years, and would be for most of the fifteen following. Despite her ambivalence about the development of the Revolution, Robinson's politics remained firmly on the side of the English Jacobins. Some of the most prominent of them were her friends: the philosopher William Godwin, as well as Mary Wollstonecraft, who would become his wife, and novelists like Mary Hays and Eliza Fenwick. All of these came from the same sort of middle-class background in which Robinson had been raised, and to which she had, financially at least, returned. Her days in high society were over by 1796, when Banastre Tarleton broke with her definitively. The stage was no longer a possibility since her physical movement was impaired, and Robinson leaned ever more heavily on her pen to make a living. In these last years she published, under a pseudonym, her only overtly political work, a short book inspired by Wollstonecraft, entitled *Letter to the Women of England, on the Injustice of Mental Subordination* (1799).

This was just one of the thirteen books Robinson wrote or published between 1792 and her death eight years later: they included novels, poetry, and two plays, in addition to the *Letter*. At the beginning of 1800, Robinson became the poetry editor for the London *Morning Post*. She was responsible for writing most of the poems that appeared there, but also oversaw the publication of works by others, among them Samuel Taylor Coleridge. Her poem "The Haunted Beach" led him to praise her meter; Wordsworth went further still and borrowed it for a poem of his own.[10] But Robinson's health was failing fast, and she, who had once made the rounds of fashionable London in her own carriage, found herself housebound on most days. She traveled in her imagination and published a series of essays in the *Morning Post* using the alter ego of a sylphid, a fairy creature that flies about town and observes the wicked and amusing doings of Londoners.

Having come full circle, let us consider more slowly what "Romanticism" means. By 1800, the artistic movement known as Romanticism was in full flower, although none of its participants would have called themselves "Romantics," for the same reason that few participants in the movements of the 1960s would have labelled themselves as part of "the 60s": names often don't stick until enough time has passed that a movement can be seen from a step back. To poets of the year 1800, "romance" would still have had echoes of its oldest meaning: tales of knights and ladies, possibly involving magic potions and King Arthur or possibly, as in Coleridge's "Kubla Khan," a Far Eastern setting. For those of Mary Robinson's generation and earlier, "romantic" meant fanciful, far-away, improbable, unconn-ected with real life.

The term also conjures up a far older artistic category, that of the sublime. When John Keats, for instance, compares his discovery of Homer's poetry with the discovery of the Pacific by (as he wrongly thought) "stout Cortez," he focuses on the sublime and awful quiet of the moment, when the Spanish conquistador and his men are struck "silent, upon a peak in Darien." While the eighteenth-century poet might, stereotypically, appreciate a beautiful spring morning in a well-tended garden, a Romantic poet, stereotypically, might prefer to struggle through a howling rain by a storm-driven sea. On the other hand, "Romantic" has also come to imply the emotion-laden power of what is domestic and quotidian. In his poetic autobiography, *The Prelude*, Wordsworth remembers himself as a small boy riding his pony near his house, watching a young woman carrying a pitcher of water on her head over a plain, her clothing tossed by the winds: "It was, in truth, / An ordinary sight: but I should need / Colours and words that are unknown to man / To paint the visionary dreariness" of the scene.[11]

While these examples show protagonists at opposite ends of the earth, one a boy on home turf and the other a man in a world totally new to him, we should notice that they are both explorers. The impulse to explore is one of the central features of the artistic movement we call Romanticism, whether the object of exploration was inward – within one's own self – or outward into unknown geography. For male writers, especially those who came from wealthy families, it was natural to imagine themselves traveling the world as explorers and adventurers. For women who had been taught that they belonged at home and that their most important job was bearing and raising children, however, exploration was a more complicated proposition.

One of the most famous instances of the Romantic brings together the domestic and the terrifying, the (apparently) feminine sphere of home, family, and motherhood, and the (apparently) masculine sphere of solitude in terra incognita – that is, *Frankenstein*, the 1818 novel by Mary Wollstonecraft's daughter, Mary Shelley. *Frankenstein* is now the most famous and most-often-read piece of Romantic literature. Much of its staying power comes from its contrasts of coziness (the scientist Victor Frankenstein's home life and college life) with pathos (the creature absorbing Western culture through conversations heard through a cottage window while he himself is shut out in the cold) and the exotic (Frankenstein's final chase of the creature across the polar ice), as well as episodes that are both familiar and terrifying: Frankenstein's weird self-education in medieval alchemy, for example, and the creation of the monster itself, bringing together childbirth and grave robbery. Indeed, if one had to point to a single distinguishing feature of Romanticism, one might say that it is the evocation of the terrifying and mysterious in the everyday.

This is not the only feature of the Romantic movement that is important in Shelley's book, however. Romantic poetry and prose are full of characters who are the victims of quotidian social injustice – legless soldiers, mistreated slaves, unmarried mothers who pine for their dead children. It was noted earlier that Mary Robinson, in her all-too-lifelike role of the suffering poet, was an ideal embodiment of one of these characters. These images owe some of their power to the eighteenth-century mode of sensibility in which the expression of emotion was given great cultural value. Sensibility translates easily to and from literature and embodied life: the pathos of Mary Robinson working through increasing pain in her Windsor Forest cottage, even her tiny funeral – at which the mourners consisted solely of the philosopher William Godwin and the poet John Wolcot – all of these made her deeply Romantic in her death. She herself emphasized the fuzziness of the border between life and literature by requesting that verses she had written for the grave of a character in one of her novels be used for her own – as they were. And we may see the influence of the Romantic point of view in the fact that even though she had earlier been castigated for her flagrantly sexual eighteenth-century persona, all of the biographical sketches that appeared in the years soon after her death lamented her as a woman who had, by her physical sufferings, repaired the damage her sexual sins had caused to the social fabric. If we still associate the Victorian era, stereotypically, with a disapproval of sexuality, we should remember that the prudery is tempered by a newly strengthened sympathy for victims and an ability to forgive transgressors.

The modern Prometheus
Mary Shelley's novel Frankenstein, or the Modern Prometheus, *with its evocation of the terrifying and mysterious in the everyday, is the most-often-read piece of Romantic literature. Its violent conjunctions still speak to us, posing questions about human nature, ethics, science, and parenthood. Frontispiece by W. Chevalier, from the London, 1831, edition.* PFORZHEIMER COLLECTION

Finally, the Romantic notion one sees most often at play in the lives of the women of this book is that self-knowledge is valuable. It is difficult to know one's self because that self is part of the mysterious world – but the knowledge is worth seeking, since it affords a lens through which one can perceive the mystery in everyday life. Often the cost of that knowledge is an uncomfortable self-consciousness by which this lens is ground and polished. Being unusual – and the women of this book, even the most retiring and polit-

ically conservative, are by definition unusual, living counter to the expectations of their day – can teach people to know who they are. Mary Robinson's many representations of herself – as poet, actress, lover, novelist, sylphid, editor – remind us of the Enlightenment belief that the self is constructed from encounters with the world; but they also evoke the Romantic ideal of the human soul that has, through painful experience, come to know itself and to be able to share itself with others. Robinson's self was a particularly rich one; as Coleridge described her to Robert Southey: "I never knew a human being with so *full* a mind – bad, good, and indifferent, I grant you, but full and overflowing."[12] Not all of the women who appear here have minds as full as Robinson's, but many of them sought and found an equally Romantic knowledge of themselves in the pages they wrote, in the romantic conquests they made, in the religions they served, in the natural phenomena they studied, in the paintings they made, in the crimes they committed, and even safe in the bosoms of their loving families. This is paradoxical, but to be an extraordinary woman in this era was – as it is still in our own – a contradictory state of affairs.

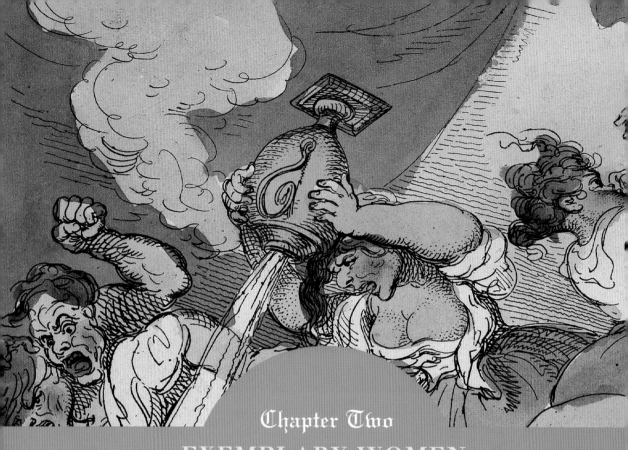

Chapter Two

EXEMPLARY WOMEN: MARY WOLLSTONECRAFT, HANNAH MORE, AND THEIR WORLDS

ALTHOUGH THEY MIGHT easily be called the most important women of their age, neither Hannah More (1745–1833) nor Mary Wollstonecraft (1759–1797) is "Romantic" in the literary sense. In the historical sense of the term, however, these women embody two political and social extremes. More has been called "the first Victorian" because of her enthusiastically religious, steadfastly conservative life.[1] She established schools for the poor, helped to launch the British campaign against slavery, and promoted evangelical Christianity. She was famous during her lifetime and into the mid-nineteenth century, but her reputation then went into eclipse; only during the last decades of the twentieth century did interest in her revive in the scholarly community. Beyond academia, her name is unlikely to be familiar to readers, although she has been credited with nothing less than leading a moral revolution in Britain.[2] She is certainly the shining example of a woman whose kind came to prominence in the late eighteenth and early nineteenth centuries: the Christian philanthropist and propagandist.

Mary Wollstonecraft, by contrast, resists definition. Her work and adult life, shaped so clearly by the French Revolution and by British reaction to it, are as emblematic of one strain of radical thought as More's are of the conservative side. She wrote a history of the French Revolution, tracts defending it and arising from it, and novels in which she tried to think through its implications for all British women. She lived by her principles, traveling much of Europe alone, and breaking, conscientiously and very selectively, the rule for respectable women against nonmarital sex. She left an unfinished life and unfinished works, dying in childbirth at age thirty-eight. But although Wollstonecraft, too, spent posthumous decades in obscurity, her fame as "the Author of *A Vindication of the Rights of Woman*" (so her widower identified her in the title of his 1798 memoir)

Mother of a movement

The groundbreaking feminist Mary Wollstonecraft is shown here in 1797, only months before her death and just pregnant with her daughter, the future Mary Wollstonecraft Godwin Shelley. Aaron Burr, the controversial third Vice President of the United States, was much impressed with Wollstonecraft's ideas for egalitarian child-rearing and brought up his daughter Theodosia on those principles. He commissioned this copy of John Opie's portrait as a gift for Theodosia. Oil on canvas by John Keenan, after Opie, 1804.
PFORZHEIMER COLLECTION

never quite disappeared. Her demands – for the rights of men as well as the rights of women – pushed beyond her present; since they have never been met, Wollstonecraft still looks into the future. So Virginia Woolf saw her in 1932: "[S]he is alive and active, she argues and experiments, we hear her voice and trace her influence even now among the living."[3] Although Hannah More placed her hopes in a future sacred state, she lived fully in her present. If Wollstonecraft is half of a female Janus head looking into the future, More looks now to the calm stasis of a well-ordered past.

More and Wollstonecraft both provoke the questions and contradictions that Britons of both sexes dealt with throughout the period: What is the right way to live one's life? What is the right balance between the emotions and the intellect? What is the proper place of women in the world? Hannah More took on the role of a Christian saint, and Mary Wollstonecraft, inspired by eighteenth-century Enlightened rationalism, the role of a philosopher-heroine; naturally, they came to different conclusions. But they were both driven by forces larger than themselves, and driven to make their fellow Britons better people than they were. This chapter will examine their lives and the causes they fought for – some very different and some surprisingly similar. Together, they show what two extraordinary women were able to make of the very ordinary choices that life initially offered them.

BEGINNINGS: "A GIRL, I WAS EDUCATED AT RANDOM"

Hannah More and Mary Wollstonecraft both began their adult lives teaching and keeping school. The five More sisters glimpsed in the last chapter had always known that their clergyman father did not have enough money to find them genteel husbands. They took strength from their numbers, and unlike Hester Darby, the elder sisters were not acting alone when they established their school, which catered to the well-to-do daughters of Bristol gentry and merchants. It was a success, providing lessons in a rather wide range of subjects – French, Italian, reading, writing, arithmetic, needlework, dancing, and singing – and flourished well after their younger sister had made her way to London to pursue a literary career. Hannah More became a pupil there at thirteen, and when she began teaching, found herself working securely with the rest of her family, supported by the community in which she had grown up. It was she who remarked that she had been "educated at random," although the phrase might have been expected to fall from the pen of Mary Wollstonecraft, whose girlhood education was genuinely random, picked up from various mediocre schools in London and Yorkshire.[4]

In 1784, Wollstonecraft founded her own school in Newington Green, a suburb of London that was new to her. Unsupported by her family,

Engraved by Ridley from a Painting by Opie

Ridley sculp

Political rivals

Hannah More (right) and Mary Wollstonecraft (left) were deeply divided in their politics, but shared an energetic and strong-willed determination to reform the world. Mary Wollstonecraft, engraving by Ridley, after John Opie, 1815. PFORZHEIMER COLLECTION; *Hannah More, anonymous engraving, ca. 1798.* PRINT COLLECTION

she had decided on a school to provide a shelter for her two younger sisters, Everina and Eliza, from the semi-poverty and unloving harshness of their family life. The unkindness – chiefly at the hands of their father, Edward – had been familiar to the sisters since infancy, and as a girl Wollstonecraft had tried to protect her mother from her father's drunken brutality. The poverty was unexpected. Edward Wollstonecraft had been a gentleman farmer, but he was a bad manager as well as a bad father, and the family fortune dwindled as his seven children grew.

As a recent biographer of Mary Wollstonecraft has noted, it was a considerable achievement for a young woman to put together an establishment in as short a time as Wollstonecraft did, with no one but her sisters and her closest friend, Fanny Blood, to help.[5] They rented a house, advertised, and found pupils as well as a few extra lodgers, in a matter of weeks. Wollstonecraft, moreover, quickly made her way into the intellectual circle of Dissenters at Newington Green, making lasting friends among the Unitarians who challenged her Anglican upbringing and taught her the pleasures of living among thoughtful, argumentative people. The school, properly attended to, might have succeeded. But when Fanny Blood, who had by then married and moved to Portugal, became pregnant and experienced a renewal of tuberculosis, Wollstonecraft sailed across the Atlantic to try to save her. While Fanny was dying, the school failed.

On her return, Wollstonecraft wrote her first book, *Thoughts on the Education of Daughters* (1787), which she filled with her own disheartening experience, writing of "unfortunate females who are left by inconsiderate parents to struggle with the world."[6] The struggle itself – with the world and with writing – must have been a welcome distraction from mourning Fanny. But one book does not pay the rent, and Wollstonecraft now had debts as well. After a year's unhappy stint as a governess in Ireland – during which she taught a willful aristocratic girl, Margaret King, later Lady Mount Cashell, who figures in Chapter Three – Wollstonecraft returned again to London. She was able to turn the experience into a book called *Original Stories from Real Life* (1788), in which the heroine, a teacher named Mrs. Mason, exercises considerable moral coercion on two spoiled girls and saves them from lives of excess emotion and narcissism. She and More had both grown up with sensibility, the late-eighteenth-century fashion for highly wrought emotions, the expression of which was felt to have ethical value: the more one wept for a kicked puppy, the better person one was. Both had kicked the habit, finding that, like laudanum (another favorite drug of the time, made from opium dissolved in alcohol, and measured in drops), emotion taken in too great a quantity left one enervated and languorous, unfit for the constant struggle that faced unmarried women.

In the autumn of 1787, Wollstonecraft entered the social and intellectual circle that was to be her emotional home for the rest of her life. Its center was her publisher, Joseph Johnson, a mild-mannered political radical who handled medical textbooks, poetry, science, philosophy, mathematics, liberal theology and sermons, and a good deal of the fiction by politically liberal novelists of the day. At his weekly dinners he hosted, among others, the artist and poet William Blake, the political thinker Thomas Paine, the novelist and educational theorist Maria Edgeworth, and Henry Fuseli, the Swiss-born artist. It was here that Wollstonecraft first met her future husband, William Godwin, a philosopher whose optimistic work promoted free love, and the idea that human life and human beings were capable of endless improvement.

Johnson's dinners were an education, but Wollstonecraft's literary work for him taught her even more than his hospitality. He gave her a variety of assignments for his journal, *The Analytical Review*, as well as book-length tasks of translating, anthologizing, and writing. Under him she learned to get to the pith of a book under review, to write quickly and convincingly, to edit the work of others, and to translate from languages she hardly knew (an important skill in the eighteenth century, when European literature was more cosmopolitan than it is now).

Hannah More, too, owed her early literary success to her ability to network and to find mentors in older, established men. Her first London mentor was no

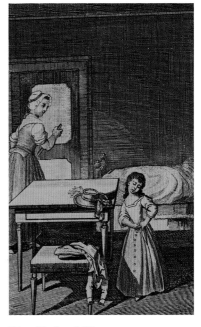

Morality for children
Mary Wollstonecraft's translation of Christian Salzmann's Elements of Morality *(London, 1791) reveals the ground she shared with the more conservative Hannah More: both promoted programs for personal improvement, starting in earliest childhood. This illustration, captioned "This slovenliness is a nasty thing," is by the poet and artist William Blake.* PFORZHEIMER COLLECTION

less than David Garrick, the most famous actor and theater manager of his day. More was not an evangelical Christian in her youth. She was, rather, in love with the British stage, and though never an actress, she was a talented writer and an extremely charming woman. Their first meeting ultimately resulted in

More's becoming the permanent houseguest of Garrick and his wife, Eva, and in the production of her tragedies at Garrick's Drury Lane Theatre. At a time when there were only three licensed theaters in London, this was no mean feat.

More began quickly to move in some high circles, befriending the aging collector and letter-writer Horace Walpole, who teasingly called her "Saint Hannah" as she became more religious.[7] But at least equally important was her connection with a group of educated (often self-educated) women, all considerably older than herself, known as the bluestockings. Chief among them were Elizabeth Montagu, a Shakespeare critic known as the "queen of the Blues" for her leading role in the group; Sarah Scott, who with Elizabeth's sister Barbara Montagu wrote the feminist utopia *Millenium Hall*; Anna Letitia Barbauld, a poet whose liberal politics and Unitarian religious views also gave her a place in Joseph Johnson's circle; and Elizabeth Carter, famed for her translations from Greek and Latin. Most of these women leaned to the conservative side of politics, and while it has become common now to speak of "bluestocking feminism," theirs was mainly practiced by intellectual adventures rather than public protests. The term "bluestocking" came to signify any woman who had learning or pretensions to learning, and by 1815 it was entirely pejorative – the women seen on the facing page in Thomas Rowlandson's misogynist caricature, fighting and spilling "French cream" (shorthand for their supposed interest in the French Revolution), are a very far cry from those More associated with at the decorous gatherings she attended in the 1770s. By the early years of the nineteenth century, More had long since left the bluestockings for more religiously minded friends; in 1801 she renounced, in print, the passion for theater that had brought her into their circle in the first place. However, her lifelong interest in women's education may be traced, not simply to her own "random" education, but also to her acquaintance with women who were serious about their own learning.

Wollstonecraft's closest brush with the circle came with her brief correspondence with the historian Catharine Macaulay Graham (1731–1791), who had known public adulation as a Whig historian of England, and public scorn when she married a man much younger than herself. In what amounts to a fan letter, Wollstonecraft wrote, in December 1790, "I respect M[rs] Mac[a]ulay Graham because she contends for laurels whilst most of her sex only seek for flowers."[8] It was a promising start, although the two writers apparently did not meet before Catharine Graham died six months later.

With her letter Mary Wollstonecraft had enclosed her *Vindication of the Rights of Men*, the polemic that made her name as a political theorist and fighter in the paper wars over the French Revolution. When the Revolution broke out in 1789, Joseph Johnson's group and many others – at first, indeed, a great part of the British populace – celebrated it as a triumph of democracy. Wollstonecraft's first *Vindication* was a reply to the parliamentarian Edmund Burke's eloquent

BREAKING UP OF THE BLUE STOCKING CLUB.

Skewering learned women

"Bluestocking" was a hackneyed pejorative for women who were learned and did not hide the fact. The melee in Thomas Rowlandson's 1815 caricature Breaking Up of the Blue Stocking Club, *in which ladies fight like fishwives and spill "French cream" (shorthand for their supposed interest in the French Revolution), is a far cry from the decorous, and rather conservative, gatherings that Hannah More had attended decades earlier.* PFORZHEIMER COLLECTION

A genteel utopia

Sarah Scott and Lady Barbara Montagu's Millenium Hall *(London, 1762) describes a genteel proto-feminist utopia hidden in the English woods, where gentlewomen engage in educational and philanthropical works. Jobs for women were a perennial problem in a world of all-male professions; yet philanthropy was an option that worked only for the upper classes.* PFORZHEIMER COLLECTION

Frontispiece.

Millenium Hall.

A DESCRIPTION of

MILLENIUM HALL,

AND THE

COUNTRY ADJACENT:

Together with the

CHARACTERS of the INHABITANTS,

And such Historical

ANECDOTES and REFLECTIONS,

AS

May excite in the READER proper Sentiments of Humanity, and lead the Mind to the Love of VIRTUE.

BY

A GENTLEMAN on his Travels.

LONDON:

Printed for J. NEWBERY, at the Bible and Sun, in St. Paul's Church-yard.

M DCC LXII.

and sentimental defense of the French monarchy, *Reflections on the Revolution in France* (1790). She propounded British versions of liberty, equality, and fraternity, writing against the inequity of rule by a small group of men blessed with inherited wealth and land, and in favor of a broad extension of the vote. The work was a success, warranting a second edition in the same year. At this point she put her name on the title page, astonishing a number of her fellow political writers who had not suspected that the author of one of the earliest replies to Burke was a woman.

Wollstonecraft then topped herself, coming out in early 1792 with the logical sequel to this effort, *A Vindication of the Rights of Woman*. This time it carried her name. In this later work Wollstonecraft does not make her sex into helpless victims. She wants them, on the contrary, to do their duty as human beings, to "effect a revolution in female manners," and thus to make them "labour by reforming themselves to reform the world."[9] She calls for women to become citizens, to move fully into the public sphere as mature, educated, self-controlled beings. What now seems paradoxical about Wollstonecraft's work is that, like More, she views motherhood as the most important object of a woman's life. But where More sees motherhood as requiring women to stay at home, Wollstonecraft sees the best mother as the one who participates fully in civic life. The *Vindication* did not come out of nowhere; antecedents by both men and women date back to the seventeenth century and even further, and whether or not Wollstonecraft knew them, she had the example of the bluestockings to show that women were capable of much more than was often required of them. Her work, in turn, inspired imitators and translations. Reviews were, on the whole, positive; the political atmosphere favored change, and if the French Revolution had not taken the turn it did, Wollstonecraft's demands might not have gone so long unanswered.

A revolutionary book

Mary Wollstonecraft's masterpiece called for women to begin the revolution at home: "It is time to effect a revolution in female manners – time to restore to them their lost dignity – and make them, as part of the human species, labour by reforming themselves to reform the world." PFORZHEIMER COLLECTION

A predecessor and role model

Mary Wollstonecraft admired the older historian Catharine Macaulay Graham, writing to her in December 1790, "You are the only female writer who I coincide in opinion with respecting the rank our sex ought to endeavour to attain in the world. I respect Mⁱˢ Mac[a]ulay Graham because she contends for laurels whilst most of her sex only seek for flowers."

PFORZHEIMER COLLECTION

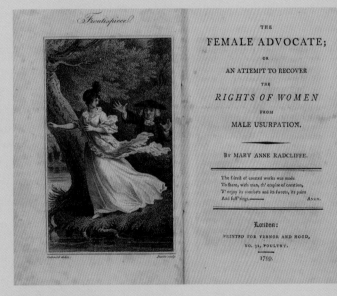

Advocate on the run

From the title The Female Advocate; or An Attempt to Recover the Rights of Women from Male Usurpation (London, 1799), one might expect the frontispiece of Mary Anne Radcliffe's Wollstonecraft-inspired work to show a strong-minded heroine; instead, the illustrator depicts a female victim fleeing from a priest.

PFORZHEIMER COLLECTION

As the Revolution continued, however, its leaders and its political tenor became more violent, and the English response first split, then fractured. Wollstonecraft and others who had supported the Revolution or its principles were reviled as "Jacobins" in much the same way that "red" was a term of contempt in the United States in the 1950s. Wollstonecraft herself was ambivalent about the events in France, and her *History of the French Revolution* makes it clear that she wished that there had been, instead, a bloodless French Reformation. By January 1793, when Louis XVI was beheaded, Britain was, for the most part, opposed to the new French regime. Wollstonecraft, then, was on the spot in Paris, working on her *History* and rethinking much of what she had known. If she was ambivalent about the Revolution, she held firmly to feminist thought, and, at last, acted on the belief that marriage was a trap by allowing herself to enter into a relationship – permanent, she thought – with an American businessman named Gilbert Imlay.

At about the same time that Wollstonecraft was writing her two *Vindications*, Hannah More was devoting her life to causes described succinctly by her friend, the evangelical politician William Wilberforce (1759–1833): "God Almighty has set before me two great objects, the suppression of the Slave Trade and the Reformation of Manners."[10] Wilberforce was the leading member of the group of scholars, clergymen, and politicians known as the Clapham Sect (after the London suburb where they lived), who were to More what Johnson's circle was to Wollstonecraft: a set of friends forming a community of belief. Unlike Wollstonecraft, who lived much of her life alone, More made a home with her four sisters for as long as they lived. Their help made possible the demanding schedule of writing, meeting, teaching, and organizing to which More felt called as her religious convictions became stronger.

Christians of More's way of thinking believed that salvation – effected by God's grace – was available to everyone who strove and asked for it. But it required constant self-examination and strict self-discipline: "in the practice of a Christian," she wrote, "self-denial is the turning-point, the specific distinction."[11] Her version of Protestantism combined belief in celestial democracy with deep social conservatism while on earth. One's duty was to be the best Christian one could, and carrying out this demand in the temporal world inevitably led to contradictions, among them that being a good Christian might lead women out of the home. More's work setting up charity schools and her writings against the slave trade had made her a highly public character. This point of entry into the public sphere, through philanthropical work, became an ever-broader path for generations of women after her. More, though, deeply believed that women did not belong in the public eye, and unlike Wilberforce and other members of the Clapham Sect, she avoided public speaking and lived in the country, not in London. She had retired, in part, to avoid the theater and other distractions from the religious life. More lived a compromise, carrying out her works of charity as privately as possible, short of complete anonymity. It was a real sacrifice for her: her earlier life as a bluestocking and playwright had taught her that she enjoyed attention. Certainly she continued to enjoy the authority she gained through charitable ventures, learning slowly that while she might be (in her own eyes) better than the irreligious gentry and wealthy farmers with whom she had to negotiate to set up her charity schools, she had still to pay some attention to their views to win her point.

The paradox of More's life was that while she believed that women belonged in the home, and that their natural profession was that of wife and mother, she also believed that women were rational creatures, and that being a good mother meant developing one's mind as fully as possible for the sake of one's children. She wanted a solid education for girls to prepare them for a life of virtue, responsibility, and good works. The first sentence of her major work on the education of young women, thus, could have come from the pen of Mary Wollstonecraft: "It is a singular injustice which is often exercised towards women, first to give them a very defective education, and then to expect from them the most undeviating purity of conduct."[12] But where Wollstonecraft, for instance, had called for girls to have room to run and play active sports, More had no wish to encourage "the hoyden, the huntress, the archer; the swinging arms, the confident address."[13] More was little interested in development for its own sake or for the individual's personal improvement. In her view, God has given life a pattern, sometimes obscure, sometimes perfectly clear, and human beings are dropped into that pattern by Providence. Within it one should be the best Christian one can, but to want to change the pattern altogether, to deny its rightness – as Wollstonecraft assuredly did – was to embrace "atrocious principles."[14]

An elderly lioness
Hannah More grew more conservative as she aged, and ever more famous. Believing that women should lead private and retired lives, she enjoyed nothing more than working in her garden, but at her cottage outside London she found herself lionized by visiting admirers. Engraving by A. Halbert, after John Opie, after 1786. PRINT COLLECTION

The implications of such thinking can be seen in More's attitudes toward slavery, which were both abolitionist and paternalist. In 1788 she had committed herself in print to the abolitionist cause with a poem called "Slavery," in which she argued for the souls of enslaved Africans: "What! does th'immortal principle within / Change with the casual colour of a skin?"[15] She dedicated considerable time and literary effort to the cause, as many middle-class women did: she boycotted slave-produced sugar; she encouraged, through her London theater connections, the production of plays with abolitionist messages; and she continued to write against the slave trade. Her patriotism was part of these efforts: since God had seen fit to allow Britain to become an empire, it now had a special duty to show the rest of the world the Christian way. We should be clear, however, on the limits of More's thought. "Abolitionism" referred to the trade in slaves, and what now seems self-evident, that *slavery* is a preventable evil, was not a common position in these years. Many white Britons believed that Africans were physically or socially inferior to them, that empire brought benefits to Africa as well as profits for themselves, and that freeing slaves outright would lead to social chaos. While she deplored the trade in slaves and saw Africans as possessing souls whose value was equal to her own, More preferred the idea of gradual emancipation and was not comfortable with portrayals of Africans who were as articulate or even as free as she was.

Her other great cause, the reformation of manners, also depended on a strong degree of paternalism. The Cheap Repository Tract series, one of the major efforts of More's life, was a purely paternalist enterprise, although it might be better called maternalist. The Tracts, written for a popular, indeed semi-literate, audience, tell the poor how to live. They feature title characters like "Diligent Dick," "Mary Wood, the House-Maid," and "Black Giles the Poacher." More wrote or edited over a hundred of them, and through her network of evangelical friends and acquaintances saw to it that they were available everywhere in Britain, to be sold cheaply or given away.

In one crucial sense, however, More was entirely egalitarian: both rich and poor needed reformation before they could be saved. Accordingly, she wrote for both ends of the economic spectrum. The rich, having been given more, have greater responsibilities, and she did not hesitate to criticize the upper classes in conduct books aimed at their souls. Mary Wollstonecraft, by contrast, saw her audience as the middle classes. The difference tells us a great deal about the two writers: however bossy she is – and she has no hesitation in telling her readers what to do – Wollstonecraft writes, most of the time, for an audience of her equals. While she describes ladies debilitated by sensibility who love their spaniels more than their children, she sees the middle class as being in "the most natural state."[16] For

More, social differences are part of God's plan and thus are worth cherishing. Her answer to the question, How should one best live one's life? was clear, though not easy: it was to be as virtuous a Christian as one could.

For Wollstonecraft the answer did not come so easily. As Virginia Woolf wrote, her life was "an experiment from the start, an attempt to make human conventions conform more closely to human needs,"[17] and she was not allowed time to work out the answers fully. When More finished work on the Cheap Repository Tracts in 1798, Wollstonecraft had been dead a year. The last few years of her life were filled with incident: after her sojourn in France and the birth of her daughter, Fanny, by Gilbert Imlay, she traveled on a business mission for him to Scandinavia with the little creature in tow. During the journey she gradually realized that she had been deserted, and when the suspicion was confirmed by news of Imlay's mistress, Wollstonecraft tried to kill herself – twice, once by drowning and once by an overdose of laudanum. Happily both attempts failed, and she turned the narrative and letters of her Scandinavian voyage into her most moving and popular book, the *Letters Written During a Short Residence in Sweden, Norway and Denmark* (1796). The letters address the ever-diminishing figure of Imlay, who fails to answer. Pathos is built into the volume's structure; as William Godwin, who became her husband in March of 1797, was to write: "If ever there was a book was calculated to make a man in love with its author, this appears to me to be the book."[18]

Lecturing to the poor
Hannah More's Cheap Repository Tracts – of which The History of Mary Wood, the House-Maid; or The Danger of False Excuses *(London, ca. 1798) is an example – were, for decades, her best-known works. Printed by the thousands, they encouraged working-class Britons to be grateful for their places. The tracts also assisted the philanthropic work of the genteel, who bought them in bulk to distribute to the poor.*
PFORZHEIMER COLLECTION

On Wollstonecraft's return to England, she and Godwin (who had first encountered each other at one of Joseph Johnson's dinners) met again, and within a few months they had fallen in love. The pair embarked on a life that promised to be full of love and cogitation, in which closeness was not allowed to become stifling. At first they did not even live together, and Wollstonecraft wrote to her husband: "I should wish you, from my soul, to be rivetted in my heart; but I do not desire to have you always at my elbow."[19] They married only when she became pregnant. Even for Mary Wollstonecraft some conventions were too strong to disobey altogether. She was snubbed all the same by some of their friends, when her marriage to Godwin made it clear that she could not have been married to Gilbert Imlay. The pregnancy ended with the birth of Mary Wollstonecraft Godwin, who would grow up to write *Frankenstein*, on August 30, 1797. Wollstonecraft had determined to have a midwife, a decision that was then both feminist and old-fashioned: male obstetricians, still called "man-midwives," were a fairly recent innovation, and women were slowly being driven out of the birthing profession. However, Wollstonecraft's post-natal recovery was slow. Eventually the physicians were called for, and after one of them attempted to remove the placenta, infection and puerperal fever set in. The infant Mary was taken away, and puppies brought in to suckle and relieve the pressure of the unconsumed breast milk. Wollstonecraft died September 10.

Hannah More outlived Mary Wollstonecraft by thirty-five years, and she continued to be a powerful social force for many of them. Perhaps the fittest way to take a final look at her thought in tandem with that of her contemporary is to compare briefly her only novel, *Coelebs in Search of a Wife* (1808), with Wollstonecraft's last attempt at the form, the unfinished *Maria, or the Wrongs of Woman* (1798). Both works set forth their authors' views of women in British society, and both are better approached as works of ideology than art. *Maria* is Wollstonecraft's catalogue, as her title indicates, of "the wrongs of woman." The setting is a private madhouse, where a middle-class woman and her working-class keeper exchange horror stories in long monologues, describing abusive husbands, employers who are rapists, competitive and unsympathetic women, and a social system that legitimates injustice. It is an accurate and dreary work with two possible endings, one in which the protagonist commits suicide, and one in which she seeks (unsuccessfully) a legal separation from her husband.

More's novel takes place in the sunshine, centering on a number of interlaced households in the English countryside. Where Wollstonecraft is insistently personal, identifying her characters only by first name and experience, More's are defined by social position. The "Coelebs" of her title looks like a name but is, in fact, a variation of the word "celibate." The novel describes a young bachelor's search for the perfect wife, an equal who is fit to share all "rational delight."[20] Since the young man, Charles, finds his beloved, Lucilla, early on, and since there is no reason why they should not be married, plot is unimportant. A great deal of time is spent admiring Lucilla's perfections: she is pious, generous, firm-minded, and learned. Since More avoids conflict or suffering, *Coelebs* is a very happy book. The good are rewarded, and a cheerful picture of England as it might be, if only everyone were better-behaved, emerges. In its day it was also very popular, selling many more copies than Wollstonecraft's feminist dystopia.

Maria and *Coelebs* have this in common, however: overblown emotion – the stuff of sensibility and some versions of Romantic literature – is seen as something to be avoided. Wollstonecraft's heroine has been crippled by sensibility, while More shows her readers the dangers of excess sentiment through secondary characters, but both authors see the value of intelligent, decisive, even strong-minded women. Like its author's reputation, *Coelebs in Search of a Wife* remained current through most of the nineteenth century, and, like its author's other works, is no longer read. Wollstonecraft's eighteenth-century nightmare, left by her death without an ending, has become a minor classic.

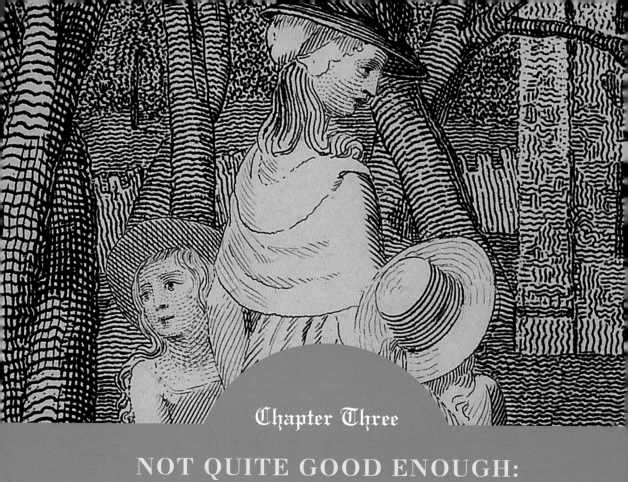

Chapter Three

NOT QUITE GOOD ENOUGH: THREE IMPERFECT LIVES

THE LAST CHAPTER looked at how Mary Wollstonecraft and Hannah More answered for themselves the question of how to live one's life. This one looks at the general answer given to girls and women: Be good! Middle-class girls of this period were raised to see motherhood as heroic, and wifehood as a profession. The gain was that they and their educations had begun to be taken seriously, although real reform in girls' education did not come until the 1870s. The cost was that education was seen as worth seeking for only two primary purposes: the pursuit of a husband and the improvement of one's children. This chapter will look at ideas of virtue through the lives of three very different women: a daughter, a mother, and a wife.

A DAUGHTER: PRINCESS CHARLOTTE (1796–1817)

Hannah More pitched her writing carefully to different audiences, and un-doubtedly her two-volume work of 1805, *Hints Towards Forming the Character of a Young Princess*, had the most select readership of all. The princess in question was Charlotte Augusta, born in 1796, the only product of the disastrous marriage of the Prince of Wales (later King George IV) and Princess (later Queen) Caroline, and, after her father, heir apparent to the throne of England. Because Charlotte was in line to be ruler of Britain, More's aim was to prepare the princess for her responsibilities to her people. Extra measures were called for: Latin, not customary for girls, was recommended, along with French and German, since these would all be helpful with history and foreign policy, while music was to be avoided since it would "lessen rather than augment the dignity of a sovereign."[1] More's ambitions for teaching the princess were not just literary; she was aiming at the open position as Princess Charlotte's tutor.[2] (The job, however, went to the Bishop of Exeter.)

If she had been appointed, she would have had her hands full. In 1805, the nine-year-old Charlotte was rarely allowed to see her parents, who loathed each other and had little time for her. She was being raised in the very small world of the royal palaces by governesses and tutors who tried unsuccessfully to instill self-discipline in their charge. Discipline from others she had in abundance: her freedom to leave the palace grounds was strictly controlled. Charlotte felt like a prisoner, and books meant for her improvement would probably have seemed only like one more method of control. When, in 1812, Dr. Fisher, the bishop-tutor, tried to engage Charlotte with Hannah More's book, she responded with asperity: "I *am not quite good enough* for that yet," she wrote to her best friend.[3] Others agreed; she was a handsome girl, but her manner was "extreme, awkward, neglected," and visitors saw her "lolling and lounging about without any self control."[4] Yet a miniature of her at eleven shows a girl unafraid to look the viewer directly in the eye; if she lacked self-control, Princess Charlotte was gifted with self-possession.

After one heroic moment in which she insisted on her own choice of husband, Princess Charlotte might have had a career as an excellent wife, but her married life, cut short by her untimely death, was so brief that there is no way to know how it would have turned out. Her parents could hardly have set a worse example. Charlotte's mother, Princess Caroline of Brunswick, was imported from Germany to marry her cousin George. She was young, lively, handsome, uneducated, coarse in her conversation, and prone to reckless acts. (Her adventures as an adulterous wife will be pursued in Chapter Four.) For his part, the Prince of Wales was interested in the marriage solely because of his debts. In 1795 these amounted to over £600,000, which Parliament might be induced to pay if he would only take a royal Protestant as a wife. He expected Caroline to live in the same household with his mistress, Lady Jersey; worse, he was already secretly married, to the Catholic commoner Maria Fitzherbert. In later years Caroline liked to say that "her only real sin had been to commit adultery with Mrs. Fitzherbert's husband."[5] Although Caroline tried to make herself appealing to her new husband, he loathed her nearly on sight and was drunk on their wedding night – drunk, in fact, at the wedding itself.[6] Charlotte, their only child, was born almost nine months to the day of their wedding. Although it had become fashionable for even wealthy women to nurse their own children, Caroline did not do so, and as Charlotte was growing up Caroline was allowed to see her daughter only about once a week. The princess's closest contacts were with her grandparents, especially her grandmother, Queen Charlotte, who was stiff and cold, and her aunts, some of whom adored the little girl.

In 1806, when Charlotte was ten, her mother underwent a "Delicate Investigation," as it was called, into the possibility that Caroline was adulterous,

A self-possessed princess
Princess Charlotte was the difficult child of far more difficult parents, Princess Caroline and the future George IV. Yet a miniature of her at eleven shows a girl boldly gazing at the viewer. The hallmark of her brief life was courage in confined situations. Richard Cosway's 1807 miniature, painted in the midst of the Napoleonic Wars, shows her already a symbol of British patriotism, the dove signifying hope for peace. Her Royal Highness the Princess Charlotte of Wales, *engraving by Francesco Bartolozzi, after Cosway.* PRINT COLLECTION

which effectively prevented the possibility that she and her daughter might ever become close. Caroline was exonerated, but the evidence showed that she had behaved very strangely, pretending to be pregnant, and sending abusive anonymous letters and pornographic images through the post to her enemies; in the words of one biographer, she was "although not clinically insane ... unquestionably unstable."[7] After this, her contact with her daughter was even further curtailed, and the enmity between her and the Prince of Wales cemented. Charlotte was well aware that she was a pawn of both her parents, but she remained loyal to her mother while her relations with her father deteriorated as she grew up and wished for more independence. She is said to have told a friend that although Caroline was bad, "she would not have become as bad as she was if my father had not been infinitely worse."[8]

Her mother was unreliable for affection or anything else, and Charlotte, although much attended to, was starved for affection in the nursery as well. She may have had attentions that she did not want, as one of her governesses, a Mrs. Udney, is said to have shown and explained pornographic drawings to her.[9] Training in virtue did not yet imply that girls should be sexually ignorant, and this was the age of the double-entendre. Writers of newspaper gossip columns used extended sexual metaphors that they expected their readers to understand. Shame derived, rather, from explicitness: Mrs. Udney's worst sin, in the reports of the time, was her willingness to *talk* to the princess about sex. When Mary Wollstonecraft claimed that we should be able to talk about our genitals with as little embarrassment as we talk about our hands or faces, and declared that purity of mind, "so far from being incompatible with knowledge, is its fairest fruit," she was herself called immodest.[10]

Far more than sex, however, the main subject of Princess Charlotte's education was politics, and if neither of her parents had much affection for her as a child, she was able to draw some emotional nourishment from the British people. She followed her father in her choice of party. The Prince of Wales had been a Whig for years, in part to distinguish himself from his own Tory father, George III. He supported the party that favored parliamentary reform, limited power for the monarchy, Catholic emancipation, and other progressive causes. But when, in 1811, the mind of the aged king finally succumbed to porphyria, his son became Regent, and with his accession to power he abandoned his former party. Charlotte found herself her father's political opponent. She wrote to her friend Mercer Elphinstone of the intended switch: "When this is known in the world ... how very unpopular it will make the Prince.... All these things must make *all good wigs tremble – but not give up, as the motto must undoubtedly be perseverance*."[11] The deficiency of her basic education shows itself in her lifelong spelling of the word as "wig."

Charlotte's position as "England's Hope" did not mean that she participated

A spunky one

Charles Williams's 1816 etching Is Not She a Spunky One – or
The Princess and the Bishop *celebrates Charlotte's famous flight
after her father tried to force her to marry. Her elderly tutor, the
Bishop of Exeter, is no match for her agility. Charlotte did not
actually run to a ship, and was soon returned to Kensington
Palace, but she held her ground and did finally marry for love.*

in political campaigns, as other women from aristocratic families did (this is discussed further in Chapter Four). Rather, she became powerful as a symbol of opposition: "[w]riting about the Regent's oppression of his daughter became a way of writing about the government's oppression of the people."[12] Charlotte's political choices suddenly became very important to the rest of the country; her father, who was no fool, kept her as much as possible out of the public spotlight to minimize that importance. The young woman – at sixteen she was approaching marriageable age – was nearly a prisoner in the royal compounds.

Personally, the habit of opposition to her father became of the greatest use to her when it was proposed in 1814 that she marry William, Prince of Orange, heir to the newly created United Netherlands. The young prince was not unattractive, and he and Charlotte liked each other. On the strength of this, the match was made. Then she read the fine print in the marriage contract. Charlotte learned that if she married William she would be expected to spend at least half of each year in the Netherlands. This was too much for a patriotic Englishwoman, and Charlotte, with a strength of character that was the female equivalent of courage under fire, broke off the match.

This was not a simple or brief process, and the treatment she received from her father as she was trying to convince him that she could not go through with it was so unpleasant and pressure-filled

A royal death
Unfortunately, Princess Charlotte's love match with Prince Leopold of Saxe-Coburg was cut short by her death giving birth to a stillborn son. Beloved as an example of royal integrity and honesty, she was mourned throughout the United Kingdom in pictures, public signs, and instant biographies such as Thomas Green's Memoirs of Her Late Royal Highness Charlotte Augusta of Wales, and of Saxe-Coburg *(London, ca. 1817–18).* PFORZHEIMER COLLECTION

that, at last, she ran away from home – that is, Warwick House – to her mother at Connaught House. The escapade lasted only about twelve hours; a train of court advisers, politicians, and attendants were sent to bring back the princess, among them the same bishop who had read Hannah More aloud to Charlotte a few years before. Her rebellion resulted in six months of exile from London; but the match was, finally, broken off.

Charlotte's marriage to Prince Leopold of Saxe-Coburg in 1816 required no heroics: although perfectly acceptable to the house of Hanover, it was also a love match. Charlotte and the very handsome German prince were unalloyedly happy, and her sudden death in November 1817, a few hours after giving birth to a stillborn son, threw England into public mourning of an unprecedented intensity. There were many sources for the grief: a young princess, a wife still in the first year of marriage, a happily expectant mother, all died at once. With the stillborn child, two heirs to the British crown, and the shining hope of the opposition, had been torn away at once.

Royal deaths are public business, with the power to arouse personal grief in everyone. The death of Charlotte was one of the most significant of the day in Britain. Her grandfather, George III, had been on the throne since 1760; both he and Queen Charlotte outlived their granddaughter. Her strength of mind had promised a great deal, and she had begun to tell the story of the virtuous wife in a new way, by showing that the good wife might have become a sympathetic royal politician.

A MOTHER: MARGARET KING MOORE, LADY MOUNT CASHELL (1771–1835)

In April 1818, in Pisa, on the coast of Tuscany, Margaret King Moore, titled Lady Mount Cashell and alias Mrs. Mason, wrote a letter for her daughters Nerina and Laura, then aged nine and three. It began "Ireland is my native land," and told the story of her life in case the girls should be orphaned at an early age.[13] The eldest daughter of a fabulously wealthy Irish aristocratic family, Margaret King had been "placed under the care of hirelings" from birth, and found the society of her parent's house "not calculated to improve my good qualities or correct my faults." Only one person of "superiour merit" had come within her circle, an "enthusiastic female" who was her governess when Margaret was fourteen to fifteen, for whom she "felt an unbounded admiration because her mind appeared more noble and her understanding more cultivated than any others I had known." The governess, although she does not name her, was Mary Wollstonecraft.

Margaret had striven to continue the moral and mental improvement begun with this woman, although she still needed advice – more, perhaps, "than those who had less exalted views."[14] In the early years of her marriage, she was active in Irish politics, supporting Ireland's freedom from British rule and Catholic emancipation from the prejudicial laws that kept Catholics from power in a country where they were the majority – despite the fact that she owed her wealth and privileges directly to these laws.

In case Laura & Nerina should be left orphans at an early age it appears right that there should be a written document to give them some idea of their Mother's story – It is for this reason I write the following pages –

Ireland is my native land – My father was Robert King Earl of Kingston, he was married very young to his relation Caroline Fitzgerald – I was the second of their twelve children & being born in that rank of life in which people are too much occupied by frivolous amusements to pay much attention to their offspring I was placed under the care of hirelings from the first moment of my birth – before three years old I was subjected to the discipline of governesses & teachers whose injudicious treatment was very disadvantageous to my temper – As I advanced in years I had various masters (for no expence was spared to make me what is called accomplished) and at a very early age I was enabled to exhibit before my mother's visitors, whose silly praises would probably have injured me much if I had not suffered so much in acquiring the means of obtaining them that they afforded me no pleasure – With this sort of education it is not extraordinary that I should have learnt a little of many things & nothing well – Various circumstances having combined to give me a premature disgust to the follies of dress, equipage & the other usual objects of female vanity, mine was early directed towards mental acquirements & at the age of seventeen I felt more flattered by a compliment to my understanding from an old clergyman than by any homage to my beauty from the most fashionable young men of the day. This might have been turned to advantage in

Margaret King had betrayed her exalted views in another way by marrying, according to her parents' wishes, the son of another aristocratic Irish family. The marriage was unhappy, and grew more so with each passing year. Nonetheless, she bore eight children to Stephen Moore, the Earl of Mount Cashell, and stayed with him until 1807 when she left her husband and children for George Tighe and, eventually, an exile's life in Italy. When she broke off her letter in 1818, she had another seventeen years to live, during which she never again saw Moore or many of the children from that first family. (Some, contrary to their father's wishes, did make contact with their mother on her infrequent visits to England.)

Our immediate interest in Lady Mount Cashell begins with her life in Italy, which allows us to ask and answer the question: How does a woman live a virtuous life when her idea of virtue is radically different from that of the times to which she belongs? Lady Mount Cashell found that such a life was possible only through complete transformation: she had to give up her name, country, class, family, possessions, and language. In exchange, she was able to live with integrity and a considerable degree of freedom. Arguably, she made choices that were more courageous – certainly they were more painful – than those Mary Wollstonecraft had made; for while Wollstonecraft had been imbued with the hopes of the French Revolution, Lady Mount Cashell lived in the more authoritarian Napoleonic era. But where Wollstonecraft was original in almost everything she did or published, Lady Mount Cashell was, with a surprising degree of consciousness, carrying through her old governess's vision. Her new name, Mrs. Mason, was taken straight from Wollstonecraft's *Original Stories from Real Life* – one of the neater turns of literary history, since the "real life" from which the original stories were drawn was that which Wollstonecraft had led in Ireland with the King family. The Mrs. Mason of the stories teaches two girls to do all the good they can in the present day, and there is little doubt that the Mrs. Mason of Pisa did the same.

The methods she found of doing good were superficially conventional. She wrote a book of advice to young mothers, composed stories for children, and translated medical treatises from the German. Her house became the local infirmary for the Italian peasants and laborers. Pedagogic writing and amateur medicine were, in themselves, normal occupations for genteel and aristocratic women. Her difference from conventional British philanthropical women was her level of expertise. While her girlhood education had emphasized the accomplishments – sewing, French, dancing, and so on – she was able to return to her studies as an adult, and, thanks to her wealth, had the time and leisure to occupy herself seriously with medicine. Mrs. Mason was rigorous, going to textbooks, rather than relying on the volumes of home remedies that were popular across Europe. Her *Advice to Young Mothers on the Physical Education of*

Children remains a model of sensitivity and good sense. She observes, for instance, in regard to girls on the brink of puberty that:

at this period of their lives ... uneasiness of mind is likely to occasion far more injury than drugs can ever remedy. The moral feelings are, often, too little considered, and the physical too much; for mothers who make no scruple of wounding a daughter's sensibility, or mortifying her pride, will yet be very ready to cram her with pills or draughts, if she happens to look pale, or complain of a head-ache.[15]

This is good advice that any teenaged daughter today would still wish her mother to follow. Apparently Mrs. Mason was able to take her own advice with her two daughters by George Tighe, who were devoted to their mother, and she to them. But there was no "happily ever after" in her life. She had cast her lot with a kind and intelligent, but essentially solitary Irish gentleman.[16] His chief interest was agronomy – he specialized in finding varieties of potato suited to Italian soil, and was nicknamed "Tatty." Although united in their love for their daughters, their relationship cooled after a few years, and they lived separate lives in the same house.

    The loss of the children of her first marriage was a bitter regret, and such a sacrifice is still difficult to comprehend, except by positing that her marriage to Stephen Moore must have been miserable indeed. She did believe that she was doing the best thing materially for her children, and their father, in any case, had every imaginable legal right over them. By a happy paradox, however, her exile allowed her to be of great service to Mary Wollstonecraft's descendants, both physical and spiritual. When Wollstonecraft's daughter, now Mary Wollstonecraft Shelley, moved to

(*Be calm, my child, remember that you must do all the good you can the present day.*

Published by J. Johnson Sept.r 1 1791.

"Do all the good you can"
This illustration by William Blake, from Mary Wollstonecraft's Original Stories from Real Life *(2nd ed., 1796), is captioned "Be calm, my child, remember that you must do all the good you can the present day." Lady Mount Cashell renamed herself Mrs. Mason, after the stories' protagonist, when she left her husband for a new life in Italy. There, she acted as physician and pharmacist to the Italian poor, taking Wollstonecraft's philanthropic advice.*
PFORZHEIMER COLLECTION

Irish patriot

As a young woman, Margaret King (later Lady Mount Cashell) was a passionate supporter of Irish freedom from English rule. She never lost her love for her native land, and in this hand-colored lithograph, from around 1833, when she was in her early sixties, she holds, as a talisman, her unpublished novel on Ireland.

PFORZHEIMER COLLECTION

OLD DANIEL and his AUDITORS.

STORIES
OF
OLD DANIEL:
— OR —
TALES
OF
WONDER AND DELIGHT.

CONTAINING
NARRATIVES OF FOREIGN COUNTRIES AND MANNERS,
AND DESIGNED AS AN INTRODUCTION TO THE
STUDY OF VOYAGES, TRAVELS, AND
HISTORY IN GENERAL.

THE THIRD EDITION.

LONDON:
PRINTED FOR M. J. GODWIN,
AT THE JUVENILE LIBRARY, NO. 41, SKINNER-STREET,
SNOW-HILL;
By B. M'Millan, Bow Street, Covent Garden.
1813.

Tales of wonder and delight

Lady Mount Cashell's Stories of Old Daniel: or Tales of Wonder and Delight *(London, 1813) was a popular children's book of the day, and carried on the Mount Cashell–Wollstonecraft connection: the publishers were Mary Wollstonecraft's widower, William Godwin, and his second wife, Mary Jane Godwin.* PFORZHEIMER COLLECTION

Pisa in 1819 with her husband, Percy Bysshe Shelley, and her stepsister Claire Clairmont, themselves exiled from respectable England, she carried a letter of introduction from her father to the former student of the mother she had lost at birth. (For more on Mary Shelley, see Chapter Five.) The link between the families had never quite been broken; Mrs. Mason had become friendly with Wollstonecraft's widower, William Godwin, in 1807 in London, and the small publishing house run by Godwin's second wife, Mary Jane, had put out her popular *Stories of Old Daniel: or Tales of Wonder and Delight* among other children's books. The families in Pisa became fast friends, and Mrs. Mason gave aid and advice to the Shelleys. To Claire Clairmont, whose position as the unmarried mother of a daughter by Lord Byron was particularly difficult, she was especially sympathetic and helpful, and Clairmont remained in correspondence with the descendants of George Tighe and Margaret King Moore into the late 1870s, long after their deaths.

Mrs. Mason, or Lady Mount Cashell, remained ambivalent about her choices and their high cost. She reflected in 1818, thinking of the early years after she had left Stephen Moore and her children, that "Misfortune must ever be the lot of those who transgress the laws of social life."[17] However, she found herself freer and, finally, "perfectly satisfied" in the hope – modest, and fulfilled – of spending the rest of her life "in that middle rank of life for which I always sighed when apparently destined to move in a higher sphere."[18]

A WIFE: CAROLINE NORTON (1808–1877)

Caroline Sheridan, like Margaret King, married for money. But where Margaret King Moore escaped from an unhappy marriage by leaving the United Kingdom, Caroline Sheridan Norton stayed to fight. Chronologically, her life extends beyond the boundaries of this book, but her version of the story of the virtuous wife warrants a place for her, since its ambiguities are redolent of the end of the Romantic era and the beginning of the Victorian. While Lady Mount Cashell made her peace with a bad marriage by a private solution, Caroline Sheridan took the more modern course of changing the law. Three episodes in her life have a special claim on our attention: the adultery trial through which her husband, George Chapple Norton, dragged her and her friend Lord Melbourne, and the two political struggles that led to the passage of the Infant Custody Bill in 1839, and the Marriage Act of 1857.

From the beginning, the Nortons were ill-matched. At the time they married, in 1827, George Norton was a conservative Tory Member of Parliament. Caroline Sheridan had grown up in a household of inherited liberal politics. Her grandfather, the playwright Richard Brinsley Sheridan, who gave Mary Robinson her start on the stage, had also been one of the leading Whig politicians of his day. But the three handsome Sheridan sisters inherited little but artistic glory and good after-dinner stories from their witty and charming grandfather. They came, however, from too good a family to open a school as the More sisters had; they needed to find husbands.

George Norton appeared in Caroline Sheridan's world wholly by chance. Still a schoolgirl, she was taken on a tour of his brother's stately home at Wonersh, in Surrey. There she met Norton's sister, and was invited to return. The girl hardly noticed Norton on her visits; they were not even introduced, but he fell in love with her and wrote a letter of proposal to her mother. It was refused – Caroline Sheridan was only sixteen – but he did not forget her. And after she had been through two London seasons without finding a hus-band, Sheridan accepted George Norton's renewed offer of marriage out of deference to her mother and desperation at the thought of being left a spinster.

A genteel crusader

In this portrait from English Laws for Women in the Nineteenth Century *(London, 1854), Caroline Norton looks pensive and serene; the depiction is completely at odds with the real life of a woman who, deprived by English statutes of any contact with her sons, vowed to change the law – and succeeded.*

PFORZHEIMER COLLECTION

Soon after they married, Norton cajoled Caroline's mother into finding him a sinecure with the government; although a barrister, he was also the heir of the estate at Wonersh, and refused to work as it was unbecoming to a gentleman. (Parliament was at this time a fine job for such a gentleman since Members were not re-munerated.) This was a bad beginning, and things grew worse: he had misled his new wife and her family as to the amount of his income, and within six months of marriage he began to beat her. Norton's abuse followed a still-familiar pattern: he would assault Caroline, then apologize abjectly and promise to reform. The law was almost useless: separations were possible, but divorce was not, except by an expensive and hard-to-obtain private act of Parliament. As we have seen, all property rights of married couples rested with the husband, and all parental rights rested with the father.

The Nortons were, nonetheless, a fashionable London couple in their public hours. Caroline Norton found comfort and distraction in society, and pursued it energetically in the late 1820s and 30s. Before marriage she had been seen, along with her sisters, as slightly coarse: "The Sheridans are much admired but are strange girls, swear and say all sorts of things to make men laugh."[19] Even after marriage she enjoyed flirtation – despite its being, as she discovered, a very dangerous game, it offered one of the few opportunities a genteel woman had to take risks or simply to play as an adult. The Nortons became friends with William Lamb, Lord Melbourne, one of the leading political figures in Britain and a Whig. Caroline Norton became especially close to him. George encouraged the friendship in the hopes of political patronage, which were fulfilled by a minor government position.

Meanwhile, Caroline Norton had begun to write poetry and novels, and gave birth to three sons. Her life was characterized by the painful duplicity common in the lives of battered women, in which to all appearances she led a normal, indeed highly successful life, while living a nightmare of uncertainty and pain at home. Everything came to a head in the spring and summer of 1836 when George Norton first left his wife, taking the three boys with him, and then instituted a suit for criminal conversation – that is, adultery – against her and Lord Melbourne, who was then the Whig Prime Minister. It threatened to bring down the government, which could not have withstood the scandal, and this may have been a factor in Norton's decision to bring the suit at that moment. But George Norton lost resoundingly. He had no evidence except the suborned word of some servants who had been fired years before. Moreover, Caroline Norton's lawyer delivered a scathing speech in which he exploded all of the testimony that had been offered. The jury did not even need to leave the jury box to come to its decision.

This would seem to have been a happy ending: the wife proven virtuous, the husband a cad, she should now have been able to get on somehow with her life. But Caroline Norton's life was transformed for the worse by the victory. Norton's loss meant that the couple could not be divorced, since the wife's adultery was the only ground acceptable to the law. And as Caroline Norton was to discover, the lawsuit had ruined her reputation. Not everyone believed the jury's verdict, and even if she had not slept with Melbourne, her acquaintance with him had reached a level of intimacy that was not acceptable for a married woman, even one whose husband was generally acknowledged to be a monster. A "ruined reputation," however, did not mean that Caroline Norton was permanently shunned by the fashionable society she loved, although she stayed aloof from it for several years. When she returned, her reception was politicized – Whig households took her in, Tories did not. Lord Melbourne was, understandably, reluctant to see the woman who had unintentionally damaged his political career.

Caroline Norton had, however, unambiguously lost the protection from slander that other women had. More than two years after the suit, for instance, the *Crim. Con. Gazette* published a character sketch titled "The Right Hon. Lord Melbourne," putting forth embarrassingly explicit sexual metaphors implicating Lord Melbourne and Mrs. Norton. And the writer asserted what had become a commonplace: "it is not sufficient to be virtuous" to maintain a spotless character. Women must also "cautiously avoid the very suspicion of being [thought] otherwise."[20] There is nothing new in this. The idea that really virtuous women must not even be, as it were, suspected of being suspicious goes back to classical Rome. But two important things had changed in the early years of the nineteenth century. The first was that Caroline Norton's shame was cast broadly by the gutter press: the *Crim. Con. Gazette* cost two pence and was aimed at a wide audience who would have known "the Honourable Mrs. Norton" as one in a panoply of public characters, someone whose poetry they had perhaps read in a Christmas annual.

The second innovation was that Caroline Norton was not going to allow the *Crim. Con. Gazette* or any other instrument of shame or embarrassment to stop her when her husband had injured her in the most painful way possible. The Nortons had separated informally after the suit, but George Norton had retained custody of their three boys. For a time he allowed his wife to visit them, but the enmity between them led him to bar all contact between the mother and children, as was his right. Like Mary Wollstonecraft, Norton fought back. But where Mary Wollstonecraft had fought in the same way that men did, through writing works of passionately reasoned political theory, Caroline Norton made the fight personal and she made it feminine. Unlike Wollstonecraft, she also managed to change the law. Norton put all of her political and publishing connections to work. She appealed to her friends in Parliament and wrote impassioned pamphlets in which she drew extensively and eloquently from her personal experiences. And in 1839 the passage of the Infant Custody Act, sponsored by Norton's friend Thomas Noon Talfourd, gave married women custody of young children.

But as in the life of Lady Mount Cashell, there was no happy ending for Caroline Norton. Norton's parliamentary lobbying was so far from disinterested that it hardly seems to have occurred to her that other women might also have been cruelly deprived of their children. Soon after Talfourd first proposed the Infant Custody Bill to Parliament, a partial reconciliation was effected between the Nortons, in which he agreed to let her have the children at times. Caroline Norton's constant pushing for the act suddenly ended, and Talfourd, who had been acting largely as a favor to her, let the bill lapse. When the reconciliation (unsurprisingly) fell apart, and George Norton once again refused to allow Caroline to see the boys, Talfourd reintroduced it at the next session of Parliament. The delay was seen as directly owing to Caroline Norton's selfishness.[21] In the event, the passage of the bill was useless to Norton; George Norton promptly took the boys to Scotland, where it did not have effect. Only when one of them had died from lockjaw after a fall from his pony did he relent and establish a regular visiting schedule.

THE CRIM·CON· GAZETTE.

No. 12.   SATURDAY, NOVEMBER 10, 1838.   PRICE TWO PENCE

PRINTED AND PUBLISHED BY GEORGE HUCKLEBRIDGE, No. 2, CHARLES STREET, HATTON GARDEN, MIDDLESEX.

THE STAGE AS A CHOICE OF A PROFESSION.

DIALOGUE BETWEEN MRS. FAUCIT AND HER NIECE MISS H. FAUCIT.

Mrs. F.—I am really both surprised and concerned, to find that a girl with your person and understanding, should think of going upon the stage.

Miss. F.—Why, Madam, it is partly on account of the former, and partly on account of the latter, that I do think of a theatrical life.—Besides, you have yourself given me sufficient reasons to have recourse to some employment for my subsistence. I cannot, indeed, expect the widow of my uncle, who left very little money at his death, should support me in idleness; and as I have, according to your own confession, a tolerable person, without which it is impossible to make a good stage-figure, I am willing to put my talents to the trial. You have also been candid enough to allow me some, which is another considerable requisite for an actress, who is desirous of making a decent appearance in any walk.

Mrs. F.—Undoubtedly it is, if any actress can make such an appearance. Every woman, who comes upon the stage, certainly hazards her reputation, though she may keep her virtue: and you are very welcome to partake of my little fortune, till you either marry, or are able to provide for yourself in a more eligible manner.

Miss. F.—As to marrying, Madam, girls with no money must not expect it; the men are either too mercenary, or too fond of their own pleasures, to take wives to share them; and in what other way can I procure a respectable subsistence.

Mrs. F.—Oh! there are several; and, were I in your situation, I should choose to settle myself in some business. You have a capacity sufficient for the Millinery branch in particular, and I dare say you have also a sufficient number of friends to employ you, and to make it worth your while.

Miss F.—A Milliner! Sure, you cannot think of any thing so contemptible for me as a Milliner's shop! Besides, Madam, the reputation of a Milliner is not, I fancy, more secure than the reputation of an actress; and if I must run the risk of losing my character, I shall choose that sort of life in which I can live in my own way, and make the best appearance.

Mrs. F.—People who are born to be dependant my dear, cannot reasonably expect to have their own way; and if a Milliner, of whom you speak with so much contempt, loses her character, it is certainly her own fault. A virtuous, discreet young woman, may render herself respectable in any station of an actress excepted.—An actress is, necessarily, exposed to so many dangerous trials, that if she is ever so chaste, and ever so prudent, she can hardly escape censure.

Miss F.—But you are inclined to allow, Madam, that it is possible for an actress to preserve her virtue; and I believe you will not deny that the most prudent woman can barely keep herself free from the blasting breath of detraction. I am conscious of not deserving the reproaches of the world, I shall give myself very little trouble about them.

Mrs. F.—Perhaps you may not: but let me tell you Helen, whatever you may think of the opinion of the world, it is of such great consequence, especially to women, that it betrays a considerable share of indelicacy to slight it.—Endeavour, therefore, my dear, girl, to get the better of a passion which, if encouraged, will certainly deprive you of the few friends you have, and be persuaded to have recourse to a more laudable employment, than the profession of an actress! an employment which, if properly attended to, will infallibly make you happy, because it will render you satisfied with yourself from the very best of all motives, from a certain assurance that you have acted right. The profession of an actress could only have been your choice from a love of idleness, sloth, and a taste of extravagance: neither of which will, I imagine, be gratified by your going upon the stage. If you will give yourself leisure for reflection, you will be ready to own with me, that the life of an actress, is a laborious one; particularly the life of a successful player: and without economy, what is to become of you when you are rendered, by any infirmities, unfit for the stage? On the other hand a steady application to business, joined with frugality, will, most probably, ensure you a comfortable as well as a reputable provision for life.

SKETCHES OF CHARACTER.—NO 12.
THE RIGHT HON. LORD MELBOURNE.

" Thus love in theatres did first improve,
And theatres are still the scene of love,
No need is there for taking on the hand,
Nor nods, nor signs, which lovers understand.
But boldly next the fair your seat provide,
Close as you can to hers, and side by side.
Pleas'd or displeas'd no matter; crowding sit:
For so the laws of public shows permit."—OVID.

Ten years intercourse with France is a more certain destruction to this island, than a septennial war. For in the time we import such cargoes of follies and absurdities, that effeminate our minds, and debilitate our bodies, that France may sooner make a conquest of England with wash-ball and hair-powder, than with military powder and ball. Not contented with the adoption of all their fancies and whimsies in dress, we follow their painted cheeks, white-lead necks, mouse-skin eyebrows, stained hair and to sum up all their conjugal infidelities. A Parisian lady only marries for rank and convenience; if she bears a son within nine months to her husband, it is likely to be his: but if not, she embraces that man who is most agreeable in the circle of her acquaintance. This our belles have progressively followed, and now an English husband, to any woman of spirit, is the dullest creature of the creation; the atmosphere he breathes in, he infects; and a pretty fellow, by way of a dangling cicisbeo, is the passion, the pride, the darling of every woman's heart. The subject of our present sketch has, in his day, been the excusee to half the married women in London, vide, his attention to the Honourable Mrs. Norton and his many court acts of politeness to Lady Brandon, all arising from the benefits of a French education; but as regards one of these ladies we may be premature in censuring her. There are more women that lose their characters with the world, who are guiltless, than guilty ones that are censured. It is the flagitious, the abandoned lewd women in hearts that is cautious of her conduct, and thereby escapes the squinting eye of defamation; but she that is unpolluted, takes freedoms publicly and gives them; and by that frankness of behaviour, is laid open to every censure and obloquy: which proves, that it is not sufficient to be virtuous, but to cautiously avoid the very suspicion of being otherwise, which we think was the case with the honourable Mrs. Norton. She could not have been blind to the amorous character of Lord Melbourne. In her heart, the reign of hymen was short indeed, for soon after the connubial knot was tied, an acquaintance with this nobleman unloosed it, and she became open to the assaults of variety. It is said that his Lordship is a great admirer of music, and plays himself remarkably well upon an antiquated piece of music called a Celestina exactly of the shape and make of a double bassoon which by the improvement and addition of a large end or top, could be tuned to the greatest nicety, in the same manner as the improved German flutes, by pulling out the end, or putting it in close. From the delicate ear of Mrs. Norton she could always keep it in tune by a shifting movement which she applied to the instrument at pleasure. This instrument is particularly constructed and is played in pieces of music set in two parts, or duets, but the manner of holding the instrument, being somewhat singular, we must be under the necessity of describing the manner in which it is played upon. Place the instrument horizontally, the end or top in a strait line, by which you have the command of it, and of course can change the tune according as the music varies. It succeeds best in such music in which the time is progressive; for instance, if the bar you begin with is a Breve, which is the longest note in music, you get a pause or rest of the same measure, and so on, occasioned by the different measures of the notes before you. It is harmonious and pleasing in any time or in any key, but it is exquisitely so when you come to quick time, which is the measure most delectable upon the Celestina. The music written in common time for this instrument has a long pause or ad libitum mark, which once he dwelt upon before you can de capo. Once when his Lordship was performing upon his double bass, or celestina, accompanied by Mrs. Norton upon the piano forte, by the effort he made to produce a fine effect, her instrument being perfectly in tune, the maid, who was likewise fond of music, upon hearing a great crash of the instruments, ran into the room, and found her mistress's piano forte had given way, by the breaking of one of the jacks. This accident was not alluded to during a late delicate investigation nor Mrs. Nortons epigrammatic elucidation of a modern husband, which she, the undying one, scrawled in the album of Lady Melbourne; drawn, since he besieged her with so many elaborately drawn, since he besieged her with so many elaborately drawn, since he besieged her with so many shoulders to all his protestations. Interest is the strongest battery that can be employed in the love sieges, and generally makes a breach by weight of metal. Jupiter changed into a golden shower, and penetrating into the tower of Danæ, as hackneyed as the fable is, furnishes very just and solid reflections. Interest, if ever the key of the heart, is the key of everything else; and the generality of lovers are fools enough to wink hard at the motive in favour of their pleasure; or mean enough to accept of it, on terms that cannot be spurned with half the contempt they deserve. His Lordship has been exceedingly liberal in this respect, as his carroll can testify, and those who are in the secret, do not hesitate to assert that he is at this very time retrenching his household expences to make amends for his prodigality with the fair sex. We have sketched him enjoying the performances at one of the theatres with one of them. It needs no ghost come from the grave to tell us who that one is. Our inimitable artist is a witch—a word—a hint—a look is enough for him and the thing is perfected in an instant. The numerous parties at the Castle and the Palace are given at the instigation of Lord Melbourne. It is somewhat singular, however, that while his Lordship is such a promoter of gaiety, (we might add) of gradation in others, he should himself afford a striking instance of domestic parsimony.

Caroline Norton's selfish mode of operating is indisputable. But if we look at some of her other actions we can see a new, distinctly Victorian, way of using femininity for political ends. Four years before the Infant Custody Bill was introduced, Norton supported the 1832 Reform Act by sending charming and flirtatious letters to Members of Parliament.[22] While the Reform Act – which broadened Britain's voting base enormously, and cleared up a great deal of political corruption – was a Whig cause, Norton could not have hoped to benefit from it personally. When she wrote "A Voice from the Factories" (1839), the first of what became a sub-genre of sentimental protests against child labor, her motivation was not merely her own enrichment. And when, as a favor to her friend Mary Wollstonecraft Shelley, she pulled strings to have William Godwin's pension continued after death for his widow, she was certainly not doing it for personal gain.

Caroline Norton in middle age

After years of separation from her husband, Caroline Norton had a brief but happy second marriage before her death in 1877. By then the laws that had made her life so difficult had largely been reformed. This photograph shows her around 1862. PFORZHEIMER COLLECTION

Caroline Norton never fully absorbed the stories of good girls. She was able to tell the story of female virtue in a way that was both new and old: old in its dependence on feminine charms and personal attachments (methods that Mary Wollstonecraft had despised), and new in its aims, which were practical, wide-ranging, and permanent. The pragmatic advantages and ideological drawbacks of her method are shown again in the passage of the act that revolutionized divorce proceedings, and significantly affected married women's property, in 1855.

This time, Caroline Norton had political competition from other women, among them Harriet Martineau, Jane Carlyle, George Eliot, and Elizabeth Barrett Browning, all of whom had signed one of the seventy petitions circulated across Britain in favor of the Married Women's Property Bill, which would have given married women's property the same legal status as that of single women. As the law stood, a husband had all rights to his wife's property (unless it had been protected in a trust), her earnings, and potential earnings. George Norton had used this as grounds to refuse to pay Caroline Norton the allowance he had settled on her after their separation, since through her writing she was able to earn substantial sums that he generously allowed her to retain. Her solution this time was both personal and public: she wrote a review of all the laws pertaining to women, but also wrote letters vindicating herself (only) to the *Times*, and published other pamphlets based on her experience as a wronged woman, one of them framed as a letter to Queen Victoria.

But she did not write, as the other women had, a new bill. Rather, she focused her attention on a bill already making its way through Parliament that would reform the divorce laws, and offered amendments to it largely aimed at protecting the property of separated women. The Married Women's Property Bill would have effected a far deeper and more thorough reform than what Norton had proposed. It is impossible to say whether or not it would have passed, since it did not come to a vote, and it was not for another decade that such a bill did pass. Meanwhile, some of the reforms that Caroline Norton had proposed – including protections for the earnings of deserted wives, and for inheritances by married women – were included in the divorce bill. They were a smaller step forward but a genuine change for the better.

What conclusions can we draw, then, about female virtue in these years? How was "being good" different then? These stories make clear that for many women, being good meant suffering: enduring the pain and dangers of childbirth, bearing the frustrations of an unloving marriage, and living with a law framed to protect men's property – all were seen as necessary to the production of good wives and mothers. Social change came from those who refused to see female suffering as a necessity. In this chapter we have seen a daughter's adolescent rebellion against her father succeed by the very traditional tactic of marriage; a mother's private combat against social rules, won at a terrible price; and the protracted, miserable war of a fierce wife and mother against a husband and the statutes of England. A broader range of women will be presented next: those who, for many different reasons, paid considerably less attention than Princess Charlotte, Margaret King Moore, or Caroline Norton did to the demands of virtue.

Chapter Four

THE MODERN VENUS, OR, IMPROPER LADIES AND OTHERS

THE PREVIOUS CHAPTER looked at women who tried, with varying degrees of success, to live according to the conventions of their time and to be what the Victorians would come to speak of as "proper ladies." This chapter will look at a group of women who were, in the public view, decidedly improper.

ARISTOCRATIC AMATEURS: GAMBLERS AND POLITICOS

The prominence of gambling in British life during the Romantic era is often forgotten, and it was by no means limited to the rich. But it was seen as a particular vice of the wealthy, who had money to throw away. Hannah More and Mary Wollstonecraft both disapproved of this "form of luxury," which was "geared not toward the display of wealth but to the display of one's insouciance in losing it," and they were far from alone in seeing gaming as an obscene waste.[1] Georgiana Cavendish, the Duchess of Devonshire, the early patron of Mary Robinson, lost the modern equivalent of over $10 million in a few months, and although she may have reacted with public insouciance, she was privately tortured by the loss. She was addicted to gambling, and lost to an extent that threatened her marriage.[2] For women there was an extra risk in gambling that did not exist for men: the possibility that one might be called upon to pay a debt with sexual favors instead of money. The Duchess escaped this fate, but it rightly inspired fear.

Some women, however, made the odds work in their favor. The popular game of faro (so called from the image of a pharaoh that appeared on one of the cards) was easily turned to the advantage of the banker, and regulations against private gaming were rarely enforced. Thus it happened that the Honorable Mrs. Albinia Hobart (1758–1816), later the Countess of Buckinghamshire, along with her friend Lady Archer, was herself the banker for a faro table.[3] In 1797 Mrs. Hobart was convicted of gaming and fined £50, then thought a lenient sentence. The Chief Justice, Lord Kenyon, had threatened even noble gamesters with the pillory, and it was widely believed that she had embezzled from her own bank. Neither verbal nor visual satirists spared her: Mary Robinson, who had been part of the circle at Mrs. Hobart's table, whipped her with words in her novel *Walsingham* (1797). James Gillray's cartoon from the same year (see page 59) shows Mrs. Hobart whipped and tied to the back of a cart – an unkind image even in an age that delighted in cruel caricatures.

The faro tables brought forth a number of images of women indulging in excess: in the midst of "deep play" (that is, for high stakes) they are shown either as uncontrollable as gamesters, or as too powerful as bankers. Toward the end of the eighteenth century, as the standards of public behavior became stricter and the sight of women gambling for large sums became unpalatable,

Ignoring the lecher

Britons of all classes and sexes loved gambling, although moralizers on both the left and right decried it. For aristocratic women, being expected to pay "debts of honor" with sexual favors was a real danger – or a viable option, depending on one's point of view. In Lady Godina's Rout – or – Peeping-Tom Spying Out Pope-Joan *(1796), James Gillray's young woman seems intent on ignoring the lecher at her shoulder.* PRINT COLLECTION

Discipline à la Kenyon.

An aristocrat in chains

In 1797 the Honorable Mrs. Albinia Hobart, later the Countess of Buckinghamshire, was convicted of gaming and fined £50, a lenient sentence. The Chief Justice, Lord Kenyon, had earlier threatened the pillory, and it was widely believed that she was also an embezzler. Neither verbal nor visual satirists spared her, least of all James Gillray, who in his Discipline à la Kenyon *shows Mrs. Hobart whipped and tied to the back of a cart.* PRINT COLLECTION

the practice diminished and the figure of the haggard woman in a silk gown, her powdered hair disheveled from her sitting up all night, staking the last farm of her husband's estate on a single card, faded from memory.

Aristocratic women did engage in more productive pursuits than throwing away their children's inheritances, and politics was one of them. It was just as dirty a game as any cardsharper played, except that buying and selling votes, and conducting campaigns by any means necessary, were the standard behavior, not the deviation. Before the 1832 Reform Bill, seats in Parliament often went to those who could buy them. Voting lasted for days, and ballots were not secret. Because of the tiny voting base (all male, and mostly landowners or well-to-do citizens), it was often feasible for candidates to visit all voters, to hold dinners for them, and to buy them beer and ale in large quantities.

The participation of women from families of Members of Parliament was traditional, and for artisan or yeoman-farmer voters, seeing the women of their local gentry for once trying to curry favor with *them* could be quite seductive.[4] But this participation also extended to non-family members, and women from the gentry up to the highest social ranks often campaigned for candidates for Parliament. Hannah More herself, in 1774, supported Edmund Burke when he was standing in the election as MP (Member of Parliament) for Bristol, though this support was limited to writing promotional pieces and presenting him with a celebratory cockade: she did not campaign publicly for him.

Despite the long tradition, conservative moralists such as More found it difficult to countenance women's public political activities. The conflict was epitomized by women's participation in the 1784 election for Westminster, an area of Greater London with an unusually large electorate. The prominent Whig politician Charles James Fox ran for one of the two seats against Sir Cecil Wray and Admiral Hood, and was aided by Georgiana, Duchess of Devonshire. It was no surprise that she would campaign for Fox; Devonshire House, her London residence, functioned as the unofficial headquarters for the Whigs, and the Duchess herself was their mentor, facilitator, patron, and friend. In 1784 she was joined by dozens of other women from aristocratic families. Fox's main opponent, Sir Cecil Wray, had the energetic Mrs. Hobart and a host of other Tory women on his side.

The campaign had national, not just local, importance, since Fox needed to win Westminster to retain control of Parliament. However, the press needs to put complex matters simply, and especially in the satirical prints – more than 300 were published – the contest was reduced to a sexual competition between Mrs. Hobart and the Duchess. The majority of the prints were against the Duchess, since they were paid for by the opposing side, and they slanted the misogynist view in many directions; Georgiana herself was made sick with despair. Hannah More infantilized her, writing to a friend: "I wish her [i.e., the Duchess's] husband

Dirty politics

Thomas Rowlandson's The Poll *memorializes the political activities of Georgiana, Duchess of Devonshire, and Mrs. Albinia Hobart, in the 1784 election for the Westminster seat in Parliament. (Another campaigner in this election, the Countess of Salisbury, is depicted on page x above as the goddess Diana.) As in many other satirical prints of the time, the political contest was reduced to a sexual competition between Mrs. Hobart (left) and the Duchess (right), shown here, for maximum offense, on a phallic seesaw.* PRINT COLLECTION

wou'd lock her up or take away her Shoes, or put her in a Corner or bestow on her some other punishment fit for naughty Children. All the windows are filled with Prints of her, some only ludicrous, others I am told seriously offensive."[5] Thomas Rowlandson's print *The Poll* (see page 61), showing Georgiana and Mrs. Hobart on a phallic seesaw, counts as both "ludicrous" and "seriously offensive." More's wish that the Duchess be shut up did not prevail, however, and Fox was victorious. The stir created by the Duchess of Devonshire was probably a substantial help in getting him elected, despite – or because of – the prints plastered on shop windows. Campaigning became more decorous in the early Victorian period, and although women did not have the vote in Britain until after the First World War, they never completely retired from politics.

ADULTERESSES

The most disturbing social errors were those that women tried to keep most private. Female sexuality in the Romantic period was a significant source of interest and anxiety. The "Modern Venus" (facing page) prefigures a shameful occurrence of 1810–15, when Sara Baartman, a similarly shaped South African woman, billed as "the Hottentot Venus," was shown half-naked to gawking Britons. The image combines satire of the push-up fashions of 1786 with the implication that women, underneath it all, are only definable through their sexuality.

This exaggeration had its roots in the fear that the old sexual mores were breaking down, and there was some grounding for it: marriage ages had dropped over the seventeenth and eighteenth centuries, and illegitimacy rates were rising, partly because of a new emphasis on romantic love and partly because of a new view of marriage as a loving, though unequal, companionate partnership.[6] Older traditions, going far back in British history, were nonetheless still very strong. The logic behind them is clear: in nations with legal systems based on the eldest son's inheritance (primogeniture), it is crucial to know that the putative father is the right one, or the property may go to a bastard. Thus laws regarding adultery and illegitimacy were much more important in daily life than they are now, and the figures described below lived, on the whole, by the double standard according to which women may not have sex outside of marriage while men, on the whole, can do what they like. The paradox of this arrangement was that rich and aristocratic women, as long as they kept their affairs and illegitimate children very few and very quiet, might have a degree of sexual freedom that was not available to women of the middle classes. Working-class women, who did not have to worry about passing on property, also sometimes had greater freedom in their choice of husbands or lovers than their genteel middle-class neighbors.

A Modern Venus,
or a Lady of the PRESENT Fashion in the state of Nature, 1786.
This is the Form, if we believe the Fair,
Of which our Ladies are, or wish they were.

An early "Hottentot Venus"

Female sexuality in the Romantic period was a significant source of interest and anxiety. A Modern Venus, or a Lady of the Present Fashion in the State of Nature (1786), based on sketches by a Miss Hoare, prefigures a shameful occurrence of the early nineteenth century when Sara Baartman, a South African woman called "the Hottentot Venus," was exhibited to Britons. The image combines satire of the pouter pigeon dress styles with the implication that women, underneath it all, are definable only through their sexuality.
PRINT COLLECTION

Ménage à trois

The beautiful and wealthy Duchess of Devonshire – portrayed here with her sister, the Viscountess Duncannon – lived in a sort of ménage à trois with her husband and his mistress, Lady Elizabeth Foster (above, right), who was first her dearest friend and their children's governess. Secretly, the Duchess conducted affairs of her own. Her Grace the Duchess of Devonshire and Viscountess Duncannon, *engraving by W. Dickinson, after Angelica Kauffmann, 1782.* PRINT COLLECTION; Lady Elizabeth Foster, *engraving by Francesco Bartolozzi, after Joshua Reynolds, 1787.* PFORZHEIMER COLLECTION

Sexuality was not in these days an easy thing to talk about: the shame often associated with the Victorian period was perhaps even stronger in the Romantic period. The difference was that prudery was not yet completely institutionalized: no one was comfortable talking about sex, but a great many people enjoyed making jokes about it. In these days, "common sense" said that women as well as men were highly sexual creatures. Many of the women in this chapter would have made bawdy jokes, and such jokes might have been made about some of them – though rarely is sexuality presented so purely as a form of amusement as it is in the two pictures reproduced on page 66.

Georgiana Spencer Cavendish, Duchess of Devonshire (1757–1806)

Marriage for love, even among the aristocracy, had become desirable by the time Georgiana Spencer married William Cavendish, the fifth Duke of Devonshire, in 1774. But where riches were at stake, marriage for love was not always possible, and the older norm of tolerated philandering survived for aristocratic ladies longer than it did for other women.

For men, the survival was much more robust. Here, again, the life of Georgiana, Duchess of Devonshire, is instructive. The Duchess brought Lady Elizabeth Foster (1758–1824) into her household as a governess. Although titled, Foster was separated from her husband and had almost no income of her own.[7] She and Georgiana were already intimate friends – "romantic friends," as their kind of relationship would later be called, meaning something between a sexual and platonic female relationship – and the hiring was a matter of kindness as much as need. Remarkably, the friendship survived even when Elizabeth Foster became the mistress to the Duke of Devonshire; the two women became allies, and he remained attached to both of them. The arrangement was difficult, especially at the beginning, and was a constant source of pain to Georgiana's mother and children. The two women shared an affection that formed, along with their bonds with their children, the emotional core of their lives.

Few women – and even fewer husbands of unfaithful wives – were so tolerant as the Duchess of Devonshire. While she was willing to share her house with her husband's mistress, she did not reveal to him her own extramarital affairs, and Foster helped Georgiana to conceal a pregnancy by a lover of her own. Elizabeth Foster became a permanent fixture in the household, and the ménage à trois lasted from 1782 until Georgiana's death in 1806, after which Foster became the next Duchess, to the consternation of the whole family – except, of course, the Duke.

SERENA.

No eye with her to cast a private glance,
O'er the dear pages of a new romance;
Eager in fictious touching scenes to find
A field to exercise her youthful mind;
The touching scenes new energy impart
On all the virtues of her feeling breast.

The privacy of home

Adam Buck's Serena *(1799) and the
anonymous* Comfort *(1815) portray women's
sexuality as a subject for comedy. Over the
course of the nineteenth century, this kind of
jocularity became less and less acceptable in
public venues.* PFORZHEIMER COLLECTION

Princess, later Queen, Caroline (1768–1821)

Beyond a doubt, the poster child of adulteresses in the Romantic era is Princess Charlotte's mother, Princess and later Queen Caroline, an extraordinary woman in a number of ways. The "Delicate Investigation" of 1806, described briefly on pages 40–41, first opened the possibility that Caroline might have committed adultery. Her innocence was declared but her character was besmirched by her undignified, unruly, and simply peculiar behavior: adopting children who might or might not have been hers, writing anonymous obscene letters to her enemies, entertaining gentlemen alone; none of this was acceptable behavior for the future queen of England. In 1814, after a formal separation had taken place, Princess Caroline left the country. She was on the road for seven years, and while her husband continued to keep mistresses in his habitual expensive style, Caroline, too, did not restrain herself. She went as far as Jerusalem, which she entered in the company of her devoted servant, Bartolomeo Bergami. The satirists could not resist the joke on Jesus' entry to Jerusalem and portrayed her on a donkey, her always-fleshy body now appearing to strain the animal's back (see page 69).

When George III died in early 1820, and the Prince of Wales, Regent for the previous nine years, finally became king, she returned to claim her due. She was presented with divorce proceedings, in the form of a "Bill of Pains and Penalties" accusing her of adultery. Transcripts of divorce and criminal conversation trials were popular licentious reading in these years. The *Crim. Con. Gazette*, in which Lord Melbourne and Mrs. Norton were seen pilloried in the last chapter, was the heir to the genre. The trial transcripts enjoyed huge sales both singly and in bound sets. George IV was not only a legendarily unfaithful husband, he was an extraordinarily unpopular king. Just as the defense of his daughter, Princess Charlotte, had been a way of promoting oppositional politics, so, too, was the defense of Queen Caroline, as radicals across the country proclaimed her innocence. Her defenders were, on the whole, well aware of her guilt, but the trial was so politicized that for many this was simply not the point. Her trial divided the country, and the failure of the proceedings was greeted with acclaim.

Caroline's role in the political fracas that surrounded her return from abroad was largely to allow herself to be made a symbol. The final battle – which she lost – came when George IV locked her out of Westminster Abbey during his coronation. Since she was legally his wife and technically innocent, there was no reason for this beyond his inveterate dislike of her. Before the event, respectable ladies registered their support of the queen by discreet processions of private carriages. Women and men of all classes and from all areas of Britain signed petitions in the same cause, and provide a glimpse of one kind of political

Versions of a queen

Princess Caroline, wife to the Prince of Wales, was acquitted of adultery charges but lived much of her life in continental Europe, far from her very unloving husband. At the death of King George III, she returned to claim her title as queen only to find herself locked out of the coronation ceremonies by her husband – now George IV. A political lightning rod, she attracted both support and opprobrium. Thus the liberal George Cruikshank portrayed her around 1820 as a dignified older woman, while Thomas Jonathan Wooler's satirical pamphlet The Kettle Abusing the Pot *(London, 1820) argues that her husband's sins are the equal of hers. On the anti-Caroline side are two scenes from travels with Bartolomeo Bergami, her courier and lover: an illustration from the anonymous* New Pilgrim's Progress *(London, 1820) embarrassingly depicts her in the bath with Bergami pouring hot water, while Theodore Lane's* A Gentle Jog into Jerusalem *(1821) shows Caroline on a donkey.* PFORZHEIMER COLLECTION

THE BATH. *on board the Polacca*

" —————— The wide sea

" Hath drops too few to wash her clean."

SHAKSPEARE.

THE weather's hot—the cabin's free!

And she's as free and hot as either!

And Berghy is as hot as she!

In short, they all are hot together!

London Pub. by G. Humphrey 27 St James's St June 3 1821

A gentle Jog into Jerusalem.
"A Saint and Courier cheek by Jowl
Set out strange Lands to see.

action undertaken by those who did not have the vote.[8] When she died in 1821, just a month after the coronation, the public outpouring of grief was nearly as extensive as it had been at the death of Princess Charlotte.[9]

Harriet Shelley (1795–1816)

If Queen Caroline very publicly made the case for the erring wife who gains sympathy because her husband's sins are so much greater than her own, Harriet Shelley, Percy Bysshe Shelley's first wife, did the same thing on a very private scale. Deserted by Shelley and pregnant by another man, she died by drowning herself in Hyde Park.[10] On her own account, she hardly deserves the epithet "extraordinary": Harriet Westbrook Shelley seems to have been a sweet, passive young woman who clung to stronger personalities. The aftermath of her death illustrates what had become a primary response to respectable women who became pregnant outside of marriage: they were victims.

Her story is brief and melancholy. Harriet Shelley's husband left her in 1814 after he fell in love with Mary Godwin, daughter of Mary Wollstonecraft and William Godwin. Harriet was only nineteen, and apparently was taken entirely by surprise when she was deserted.[11] The little correspondence that we have from her between 1814 and her death is depressed; she began, as well, to spread rumors that Godwin had sold his daughter to P. B. Shelley. She left behind two children by Shelley, and was heavily pregnant with another man's child at the time of her death. At the coroner's inquest, her landlady's maidservant reported that she had seen "nothing but what was proper in her Conduct with the exception of a continual lowness of Spirits."[12]

Harriet Shelley left a suicide note but did not mention her pregnancy, writing instead: "why should I drag on a miserable existence embittered by past recollections & not one ray of hope to rest on for the future."[13] While the public press could be venomous in its attacks, it could also be protective, and in this case it was. When Frances Imlay Godwin, Mary Wollstonecraft's daughter by Gilbert Imlay, killed herself by an overdose of laudanum at an inn in Swansea shortly before Harriet Shelley's death, her identity too was protected by the law and the press. In both cases the women were portrayed as the antithesis of the lustful woman: they were victims, a pathetic stereotype that became ever more prevalent in the Romantic period; by the time Victoria reached the throne, it was the standard way to speak of errant young women, not only those from middle-class families but working-class women as well, including the ones who turned to prostitution. The image of the victim allowed respectable men and women to feel pity for prostitutes, and also strengthened the still-novel idea that proper women were naturally mothers and should not enjoy sex.

To you my dear Sister I leave all my things as they more properly belong to you than any one ... My dearest ... Sister

When you read this ... I shall be no more an inhabitant of this miserable world ... do not regret the loss ... Why should I drag on a miserable existence embittered by past recollections & not one ray of hope to rest on for the future. The remembrance of all your kindness which I have so unworthily repaid has often made my heart ache ... I know that you will forgive me ...

"Why should I drag on a miserable existence embittered by past recollections & not one ray of hope to rest on for the future." – so wrote Harriet Westbrook Shelley in the suicide note she left on December 7, 1816, before drowning herself in Hyde Park. The first wife to the poet Percy Bysshe Shelley, Harriet became pregnant by another man after her husband deserted her. The press portrayed her as a pathetic victim, a stereotype that became ever more important in the Romantic period, as the unattributed novel Domestic Misery, or The Victim of Seduction (London, 1802) – one of many of its kind – attests. PFORZHEIMER COLLECTION

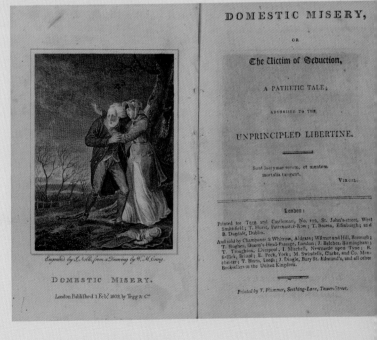

Engraved by L. Nell, from a Drawing by H. M. Craig.

DOMESTIC MISERY.

London Published 1 Feby. 1803, by Tegg & Co.

DOMESTIC MISERY,

OR

The Victim of Seduction,

A PATHETIC TALE;

ADDRESSED TO THE

UNPRINCIPLED LIBERTINE.

Sunt lacrymæ rerum, et mentem
mortalia tangunt.

VIRGIL.

London:

Printed for Tegg and Castleman, No. 122, St. John's-street, West Smithfield; T. Hurst, Paternoster-Row; T. Brown, Edinburgh; and B. Dugdale, Dublin.

And sold by Champante & Whitrow, Aldgate; Wilmot and Hill, Borough; T. Hughes, Ludgate-Hill; J. Belcher, Birmingham; T. Troughton, Liverpool; I. Mitchell, Newcastle upon Tyne; B. S-llick, Bristol; E. Peck, York; M. Swindells, Clarke, and Co. Manchester; T. Binns, Leeds; J. Dingle, Bury St. Edmund's, and all other Booksellers in the United Kingdom.

Printed by T. Plummer, Seething-Lane, Tower-Street.

Prostitutes as victims

Thomas Rowlandson's The Last Shift, *depicting a young prostitute at the pawnbroker's, uses an old pun – a "shift" was a slip or petticoat that one might pawn for a few pence, but a "last shift" was also a "last resort." In both cases the emphasis is on the prostitute as victim of society, although this young woman looks rather cheerful.* PRINT COLLECTION

LADIES TRADING ON THEIR OWN BOTTOM.

Prostitutes as predators

The traditional presentation of prostitutes as greedy and deceitful was also still viable in the Romantic period, especially in conjunction with other stereotypes, such as this anti-Semitic portrayal of a Jew in Thomas Rowlandson's Ladies Trading on Their Own Bottom *(ca. 1810).* PRINT COLLECTION

Some women conducted active sexual lives outside of marriage but refused the label of victim. Courtesans were first among them. Being a courtesan was a more complicated matter than it might seem at first blush: courtesans were usually attached to one man (though they might change men quite often), from whom they often received a fixed allowance. It did mean, however, that one lived as an unabashedly sexual creature, and the lower down the economic scale one found oneself, the more unabashed one had to be. Outright prostitutes, such as the women shown here in a print that panders to both the misogynist and anti-Semitic strains of British culture, would gather in certain areas of London, and accost by voice and by touch all male passers-by.

Yet courtesans were not shameless. On the contrary, they made genteel men comfortable because they were not totally unlike the women the men knew in their aboveboard social worlds. Courtesans lived just over the boundary of respectability, and while many stayed on the disreputable side, a few were able, even as the boundary became harder to cross, to transform themselves into wives.

Harriette Wilson (1786–1845)

Harriette Wilson, one of the most successful courtesans, parlayed her sexual history into a bestseller: the *Memoirs of Harriette Wilson* went through thirty-five editions in the first year of publication. It constitutes one of the rare pieces of blackmail that might also be called charming. Wilson's success began with her talent for writing: she sometimes found keepers – as men who supported mistresses were called – by introducing herself to men through impudent but seductive notes. This was only at the precocious beginning of her career; once launched, she was, for years, in the keeping of one man or another, gadding about from the newly fashionable beach resort of Brighton, down to London, over to the Continent. She was beautiful, but more important, she had the two requisite skills of a courtesan: she was good company and she liked sex. Many of her lovers were aristocrats or important politicians. Thus, when the time came to write her memoirs, she had a string of well-known names and addresses.

Wilson's publisher, John Joseph Stockdale (whose private life took the same evangelical path that Hannah More's did), hit on an ingenious method of bringing out the *Memoirs*: they were published in parts, with a new installment each month.[14] This offered Wilson time to negotiate with – that is, blackmail – the men whose names and adventures were about to be made public. Generally she asked for an annuity of £20 to £40, or a lump sum of £200, in return for which

The tactful mistress

*The courtesan Harriette Wilson blackmailed former lovers –
many of them rich and respectable – who wanted to keep
their names out of her* Memoirs *(London, 1825), which was
issued in installments, giving her time to negotiate. Even
when she named names, however, she was suggestive rather
than graphic, an oversight some of her illustrators tried to
address with racy pictures, such as the one reproduced here.*

she would refrain from naming their names. Some men bargained; some paid; some, as the Duke of Wellington is said to have done, replied "Write and be damned!"[15] Ultimately, Wellington's was the sensible position, since for men willing to wait out the gossip there was no lasting social penalty. But men as well as women knew what shame was, and when it is difficult to talk about sex in a serious way, it is easy to talk about it in a damaging way.

Wilson did publish, and her *Memoirs* sold – and sold, and then sold some more. There was no copyright protection for works such as hers, and the pirate publishers who flourished in those years started printing cheap versions of the *Memoirs* as soon as they could. Besides pirates, libel suits might have been the great danger. Finally, however, none of the men named wanted to exacerbate the publicity or rehearse sordid tales in court by suing.

Suing would have been particularly self-defeating because Wilson's accounts are by no means explicit. Sex sold the *Memoirs*, but Harriette Wilson's business was to tease, and she omitted all details on her lovers' styles or activities in bed.[16] She relied instead on an insouciant, thoroughly disarming style, opening her book, for instance: "I shall not say why and how I became, at the age of fifteen, the mistress of the Earl of Craven. Whether it was love, or the severity of my father, the depravity of my own heart or the winning arts of the noble Lord ... does not now much signify; or if it does, I am not in the humor to gratify curiosity in this manner."[17]

Insouciance was the appearance Wilson tried to give her whole life. She was not used to saving, and rapidly fell afoul of one of the most serious and now nearly forgotten plagues of the Romantic period (and long before): debt. It was easy to find oneself arrested for debts, even small ones, and difficult to get out of prison. Wilson eventually availed herself of the most effective way to avoid debtors' prison, which was to move to France. She died alone in Paris, abandoned by the man she had called her husband. But she did not die quite forgotten, and her fundamental good nature allowed her to count on a certain amount of affection from some unlikely candidates. In one of her last letters, she asked a former lover, the politician Henry Brougham, now in the House of Lords, to pay for her funeral, along with the Dukes of Leinster and Beaufort. All of them had at one time paid her hush money, but she hoped they would let bygones be bygones. She had totted up the costs of her very modest interment and threw herself on their goodwill. And she was right: one last time, for a now permanently silent Harriette Wilson, they paid.

Emma Hamilton's lithe youth

As the mistress of Sir William Hamilton, Emma Hart became famous for her "attitudes," in which she posed as figures drawn from classical art and mythology – here she is a Bacchante, a frenzied female worshipper of Bacchus, the god of wine. Engraving by Tommaso Piroli, after Frederick Rehberg, from Drawings Faithfully Copied from Nature at Naples *(Rome, 1794).* PRINT COLLECTION

A gift for theater

By 1801 Emma had become Lady Hamilton; she was now also the rather ample mistress of her husband's great friend, Horatio, Lord Nelson. In Dido in Despair! *(1801), James Gillray attacked her melodramatic tendencies, taking the opportunity to show off his particular talent for drawing hands.* PRINT COLLECTION

Emma Hamilton (1761?–1815)

Emma Hamilton, most famous of all the mistresses of the period, crossed into respectability without giving up her fondness for public performance, and her paradoxical position has fascinated readers ever since. Making multiple transformations of her life, she became a wife, a mistress, and, not least, a series of theatrical presentations known as "attitudes." Born Amy Lyon, she grew up in Wales, nearly illiterate and very beautiful. It seems likely that she spent some time as a prostitute in London, but one of the secrets of her later self-transformation was that she did not discuss her youth, and while rumors abounded, she did not respond to them. However, by twenty-one she had become the mistress to a young politician named Charles Greville, second son to the Earl of Warwick. Greville had fallen into debt, and Emma helped him to economize, keeping house for him in a quiet part of London. She had a daughter and strove to improve her education. Greville's friend, the celebrated portraitist George Romney, who adored her chastely, painted her often. As lives of sin go, it was retired and peaceful.

Greville, however, dreamed of finding an heiress to marry, and Emma Hart – as she was now called – was an impediment to this goal. His tasteless solution was to offer her to his uncle, Sir William Hamilton, the British ambassador to Naples, in hopes that providing him with a mistress who was beautiful, faithful, and highly domesticated would influence him in his money-lending capacities. It was crass, but proved a correct calculation.

Greville had not factored in the possibility that the relationship between Emma and his uncle might one day include love. Emma met Sir William in 1784, and went to Naples in 1786, horrified, at first, to discover that he expected her to become his mistress. Greville encouraged her, however, and she eventually gave in. She married Hamilton in 1791. Greville, who never did capture his heiress, found some help forthcoming from his uncle. Meanwhile, Emma had effected an Eliza Doolittle–like transformation in real life. She learned Italian and took singing lessons for a voice that turned out to be extraordinarily beautiful. After her marriage she was introduced into Neapolitan and British society. She became intimate with the queen of Naples, an important figure in the sticky web of diplomacy during the Napoleonic Wars, and used her friendship to promote British interests in Italy. She learned how to entertain on a large scale and how to charm very different kinds of people. Amy Lyon had become Lady Hamilton, a diplomatic wife.

She had also begun to enthrall Sir William and his guests with her famous "attitudes." To "take an attitude" was to strike a dramatic pose derived from a work of art, and those Emma took on were often imitations of figures from the Greek and Roman sculptures, coins, and vases that Sir William loved. (Many wealthy Englishmen collected such objects in these years, and Hamilton's collection was legendary.) The attitudes were admired for nearly the rest of her life, for "notwithstanding her enormous size," she continued to perform them at least until 1805, when she was in her mid-forties.[18]

Horatio, Lord Nelson, at the time he became acquainted with Emma Hamilton in 1798, had just won the Battle of the Nile, in which Napoleon's fleet was turned aside from its mission in Egypt. By this time Lady Hamilton was the leading hostess of Naples, and she put on a celebration for Nelson befitting the crucial victory. He became, besides Emma Hamilton's lover, the dearest friend of her husband, and the two of them concealed their affair so carefully that all three maintained an intimate friendship. For such performances to succeed, all of them had to believe in their parts at least to some degree, and it is clear that in this relationship (a variation on the one shared by the Duke and Duchess of Devonshire and Elizabeth Foster) there was love on all sides. Despite this, London society, to which they had all returned soon before Sir William's death, looked askance at Lady Hamilton, and the reputation she had so slowly built up in Naples began to deteriorate again.

Sir William Hamilton died in 1803, aged seventy-two, with Nelson at his bedside and Emma holding him; they mourned him with unfeigned grief. Nelson, however, was still a married man. Although he adored Horatia, the daughter born to Emma while Sir William still lived, there was little he could do for his beloved mistress beyond petitioning the government for a pension in return for her services to Britain. Their affair was ended abruptly by his death at the Battle of Trafalgar in 1805, where his last thoughts were of Emma. In later years, Emma Hamilton, whose gift for theater had veered to the melodramatic, would faint away at theaters when the song "Rest, Warrior, Rest," was played.[19] Her own ending was more pitiful than melodramatic: although both Hamilton and Nelson had left her legacies, neither was adequate to keep up with her expenses, since she had learned how to spend like an aristocrat. She had gained, more or less, sexual respectability but had lost the frugal domestic touch she had learned with Charles Greville. Like Harriette Wilson, Emma Hamilton died in debt, attended by her daughter Horatia.

ACTRESSES

The Romantic period is the last in Britain for which a chapter on "improper women" might be the right place for actresses. Since the entrance of women on the professional stage in 1661, actresses had been seen as little more than high-class prostitutes. But during the Romantic era, the cult of the star came into being. The popularity of the theater helped to legitimize the profession. In these years, for the first time, actresses could be counted among respectable women –

if they worked hard at it, and made no false steps into gentlemen's beds. For some women – Mary Robinson, for example, or Dora Jordan, soon to be described – charm and glamour might be enough to secure the affection of audiences even if one had foregone one's good name. But being an actress no longer in itself meant that one had done so.

Sarah Siddons (1755–1831)

Mrs. Siddons's name, for theater fans, is still that of a star. Besides David Garrick, whose career ended just as hers was beginning, no actor came close to Sarah Siddons in fame or popularity on the stage at this time. Her career was built on her versatility in different tragic roles and the operatic intensity of her performances.

Siddons was born into an acting family: she was the sister of Charles and John Philip Kemble, and the aunt of Fanny Kemble, all renowned actors in their own right. This gave her an insider's beginning, but her career was built on hard work. Actors trained for the London stage by working in the British provinces with touring theater troupes, and Siddons spent years touring. Her apprenticeship included a false start in London when, after what she thought was a successful season, she was dropped from the rolls of Drury Lane. She returned to the provinces, and by 1782 her performances were selling out regularly in Dublin and Edinburgh in the summers. She worked during the year at the theater in the fashionable spa-town of Bath. At this point she returned to London and found herself, as sometimes happens, suddenly famous after years of work.

Siddons maintained her popularity, in part, by keeping up her reputation as a wife and mother. At her last performance in Bath on the way to the big time of London, she brought her children on stage to show why she was leaving: there were few jobs for women in these years, but earning for the sake of one's children always evoked pity and respect in an audience. And she had a reputation as a prude: it was said that she would not pronounce the word "lover" on stage, and her brother John Philip Kemble rewrote some of her parts for her to avoid sexual impropriety. Nor would she play Cleopatra, the only important tragic female role in Shakespeare that she refused, because the Egyptian queen's sexuality was too brazen. Although she would play the parts of pitiable fallen women, Siddons "invested a dignity in each of these characters that transcended their sexual indiscretions."[20] She avoided playing the cross-dressing breeches roles that showed off legs and were indisputably sexy. In the many portraits of her, artists stressed her dignity as an artist or as a woman. She was careful about the company she kept, cultivating a middle-class and gentry circle of friends, including the novelist Frances Burney.

Mrs. Siddons

*Known for the operatic intensity of her
performances, Sarah Siddons maintained a
reputation as a loving wife and mother as
well as something of a prude. In the many
portraits of her – such as this one of her in
the role of Zara from Aaron Hill's play of
the same name – artists usually stressed her
dignity, but her reputation for greed gave
James Gillray the ammunition to portray
her reaching for bags of money as she lets
the symbols of the tragic actress – a dagger
and a goblet of poison – fall to the ground.
James Gillray,* Melpomene [Mrs. Siddons],
1784; Mrs. Siddons in the Character of
Zara, *mezzotint by J. R. Smith, after Thomas
Lawrence, 1783.* PRINT COLLECTION

None of this was enough to save Siddons from one sort of attack, which may have arisen, indeed, out of her being so careful for her family's welfare. She was reputed to be greedy – even to be uncharitable toward her fellow actors, at a time when acting was a much worse remunerated profession than it is now. There was little truth to these rumors, but they succeeded in stopping a few of her performances in the mid-1780s. It was true that Siddons was the primary breadwinner for her large family. It was also true that Richard Brinsley Sheridan, playwright, politician, manager of the Drury Lane Theatre (and grandfather to Caroline Norton), often neglected her pay, although she was not alone in finding her money late from Sheridan. However, satirists are not in the business of being magnanimous to their targets, and James Gillray portrayed Siddons in 1784 reaching for bags of money as she lets the symbols of the tragic actress – a dagger and a goblet of poison – fall to the ground (see opposite).

This was hardly the end of her career: Sarah Siddons continued performing regularly until 1812, several times acting as reader to the royal princesses, the elder daughters of George III, for the improvement of their taste and elocution. Unsurprisingly, Siddons was very far from being in debt when she died, and left an estate of over £50,000. She also left a permanently improved workplace for women in the acting profession and a new understanding that a woman could be an artist on the stage as well as something approaching a courtesan.

Dorothy Jordan (1761–1816)

Dorothy (Dora) Jordan had no such pretenses to virtue, but where Sarah Siddons was the primary tragedienne of her generation, Jordan was the most important comedienne, gaining a great deal of affection from her audiences by her performances of the breeches roles. Audiences knew her as "Little Pickles," the name of one of her most popular parts, though she was also known more respectfully as Mrs. Jordan. Not least, she was known for close to twenty years as the mistress to William, Duke of Clarence, later King William IV.

Dora Jordan bore ten children to the Duke, all surnamed FitzClarence. Any relationship of such length and fertility is tantamount to a marriage, and both Jordan and the Duke were devoted to their children. Legal marriage, though, was not a possibility: the Duke could not marry a commoner, and Dora Jordan, herself illegitimate, was already the mother of two children out of wedlock. However, the stability and affection of the arrangement gave it a social legitimacy that may seem surprising; Princess Charlotte, for instance, went riding with one of the FitzClarence boys and wrote of Jordan to the Duke as "a true friend" and "a most affectionate mother."[21] James Gillray produced a caricature showing the Duke and Dora promenading to Bushy, their home (see page 83).

Mrs. Jordan

Dorothy – known as Dora – Jordan was the most important comedienne of her day, as well as the mistress for close to twenty years of William, Duke of Clarence. Her gamine appeal shines out from the portrait of her as Hypolita, one of the cross-dressing roles for which she was famous. Jordan bore ten children to the Duke, and James Gillray's caricature satirizes the family on a stroll. After the Duke's unwilling separation from Mrs. Jordan, he continued to take an interest in his family, as shown in this 1812 letter beginning "I have found all the dear children quite well." Hypolita, *engraving by John Jones, after John Hoppner, 1791.* PRINT COLLECTION; *James Gillray,* La Promenade en Famille – A Sketch from Life, *1797.* PRINT COLLECTION; *autograph letter from William, Duke of Clarence to Dora Jordan, September 25, 1812.* PFORZHEIMER COLLECTION

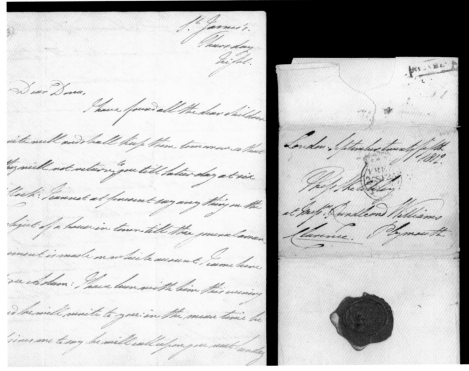

While the Duke is red and puffs with exertion as he pulls his little monsters, Dora Jordan is poised and dignified, if somewhat inattentive as she learns her lines. In 1811, however, this placid situation came to an end. The royal family realized that they had a scarcity of legitimate offspring, and the Duke of Clarence broke off with Mrs. Jordan to marry.

By then it was impossible to assault a woman generally acknowledged as one of the great performers of her generation and a dedicated mother. So when, in 1813, the *Times* of London published a scathing denunciation of Dorothy Jordan soon after urgent financial need forced her back on stage, it did not go unanswered. The attack claimed that she brought shame to the stage and double shame to the Duke, who could have "sent her back to penitence and obscurity" for daring to act in public once again. But the public was by no means in accord with the *Times*, always a stodgy newspaper and then under a particularly conservative editorship. The night after the piece was published, the audience at Jordan's performance "shouted its applause ... until the tears came to her eyes" when one of the characters recited the line "You have an honest face and need not be ashamed of showing it anywhere."[22] Jordan herself replied to the *Times* with a widely reprinted and admired defense – not of herself, but of the Duke of Clarence, against whom unfair charges had also been made. She did not deign to reply to the charges made against her personally. Mrs. Jordan had returned to the stage because of debt caused by her son-in-law's fiscal mismanagement, rather than her own. She died in France, unexpectedly, three years later, her life an illustration of how talent and good nature can make inroads against even the most rigid social conventions.

FEMALE HUSBANDS AND ROMANTIC FRIENDS

Although there was no developed lesbian culture of the kind one finds now in many countries, lesbians in the Romantic period were not such "impossibilities" as Queen Victoria is reputed to have thought them.[23] The evidence of lesbian life in the Romantic period shows us one final way women could make a name for themselves as improper women – but it also shows ladies who achieved adulation and fame simply for living as they wished to.

For women who loved other women, or just liked them a lot, the best evidence we have is from scurrilous and defamatory documents. Most of these start from the ancient assumption that sex without a penis simply isn't sex. Logically, then, women who are attracted to other women are, in some sense, men manqués, who have to make up their deficiencies by artificial means. And indeed this is what we see in eighteenth-century Britain. Mary Hamilton is one of the best-known "female husbands" – women who dressed and passed as

Exposed

For centuries, British songs had described young women dressing as sailor boys or soldier laddies to seek their sweethearts – as well as adventures that were otherwise impossible for girls. The ballads always included an amusing or moving scene of discovery, one of which is shown here in a French take on the tradition. In real life, women who cross-dressed, especially to seduce other women, were often tried for fraud. Lindor et Clara, II, *engraving by F. Bonfoy, after Francis Wheatley, ca. 1785.*

Portrait of
ABIGAIL ALLEN

Portrait of
THE FEMALE HUSBAND!

Chaste union?

An 1829 pamphlet offered a somewhat naive view of same-sex marriage, claiming that the "female husband," James Allen, maintained the disguise of masculinity by entirely avoiding physical contact with his wife, Abigail, during twenty-one years of marriage (James's physical gender was discovered only after death). These drawings of the couple are from An Authentic Narrative of the Extraordinary Career of James Allen, the Female Husband *(London, 1829).* PFORZHEIMER COLLECTION

MARY HAMILTON

THE
SURPRISING ADVENTURES
OF A
FEMALE HUSBA[ND]
CONTAINING,
The whimsical Amours, curious Incid[ents]
AND
DIABOLICAL TRICKS
OF
Miss M. Hamilton, alias Mr. G. Ham[ilton]
ALIAS
Minister Bently, alias Doctor O'Kee[fe]
ALIAS
Mrs. Knight, the Midwife, &c.
WHO
MARRIED THREE WIV[ES]
And lived with each sometime undiscovered,
FOR WHICH ACTS,
She was tried at the Summer Session[s]
In the County of Somerset in the Year 1752.
FOUND GUILTY,
And whipped four several times, in four Market T[owns]
And afterwards Imprisoned Six Months;
Notwithstanding which,
On the Evening of the first Day of her Exposur[e]
she attempted to bribe the Goaler to procure her
young Girl to gratify her most monstrous and
Unnatural Propensity.

LONDON:
Printed by J. BAILEY, 116, Chancery-Lane, L[ondon]
PRICE 6d.

The Prisoner being convicted of this base and scandalous crime was sentenced to be publicly and severely whipped four several times in 4 Market Towns, and to be imprisoned for 6 Months. vide page 21.

Denunciation and titillation

The Surprising Adventures of a Female Husband, *describing the trial of Mary Hamilton – written by none other than the novelist Henry Fielding and first published in 1746 – was reprinted in 1813, at the height of the British Romantic era. In this pamphlet, Fielding, in a humorously titillating style, denounces Mary Hamilton's marriage to another woman as unnatural.*
PFORZHEIMER COLLECTION

men, married other women, and used a dildo or some other device to have sex with their wives.

A long European tradition of cross-dressing women existed, and reasons to pass as a man were as likely to be economic as sexual.[24] In Britain, indisputably heterosexual women who disguised themselves as soldiers or sailors to follow their sweethearts into war were celebrated in ballads and prints. When female husbands were discovered, however, they were tried as frauds or vagrants. Mary Hamilton would not be remembered today except that the novelist Henry Fielding, also a judge in London, wrote a pamphlet telling her story using, apparently, "13% facts" (and by calculation, 87% fiction).[25] Fielding's original pamphlet came out in 1746, and denounces Mary Hamilton's marriage to another woman as unnatural, although the situation is also meant to titillate the reader.

For our purposes, the most interesting aspect of Mary Hamilton's case is that the pamphlet was reprinted at the height of the British Romantic era. The edition illustrated here dates from about 1813, with a frontispiece catering to the British taste for flogging. While the original Mary Hamilton was described as merely using a dildo to satisfy her wife, the 1813 Mary Hamilton has become a "traveling saleswoman of her specialized wares."[26] Despite its coarseness, the frontispiece is meant to amuse; lesbians here are naughty, perverse even, but they are still sexual beings.

The 1829 pamphlet *An Authentic Narrative of the Extraordinary Career of James Allen, the Female Husband*, by contrast, has lost its sense of humor. James and his wife, Abigail, look soberly at each other in the drawings reproduced here. The writer's main point is to convince the reader that for twenty-one years James Allen kept up the pretense of masculinity by the total avoidance of contact with Abigail. Not only has the dildo disappeared but so has all physical affection. We should probably not interpret this to mean that British prudery blossomed between 1813 and 1829; rather, we should read these pamphlets together as evidence that sexuality in the nineteenth century was then, as it is now, the subject of a very wide range of opinions.

Becoming a female husband was not the only way for women to express love for each other in the Romantic era. Another possibility existed then that is now largely lost to us: romantic friendship, a tender coupling off that formed an alternative to marriage for a few women, and that was enjoyed in a less extreme form by many more. Lady Eleanor Butler (1739–1829) and Sarah Ponsonby (1755–1831), the most famous pair of romantic friends, were in their heyday in 1813.

The Ladies of Llangollen,[27] as they were known, came from old Irish families, with Eleanor Butler the older and more determined of the two. While still in Ireland they became friends and, finding their families immovably opposed to their desire to spend their lives together, eloped, taking a tour of romantic and mountainous Northern Wales. In 1780 they settled there in Llangollen, finding a little cottage, Plas Newydd, where they could spend their lives in retirement. This consisted primarily of quiet activities: reading, writing, studying, keeping accounts – as the ladies said, most of their pleasures had to do with paper. Many of the others took place in the sedulously tended gardens, planned according to the taste of the day for the picturesque and the gothic. There were shaded garden seats for reading, but the ladies were full of energy, and recorded in their journal running "round the garden in the freezing rain," and coming in to enjoy the blazing fire afterward.[28]

Romantic friends

The most famous example of a loving and intimate companionship is that of Lady Eleanor Butler and Sarah Ponsonby, an Irish couple who were in their heyday in 1813. Known as the Ladies of Llangollen, the charismatic pair attracted visitors such as William Wordsworth, Sir Walter Scott, the writer Mme de Genlis, the scientist Sir Humphry Davy, the young Charles Darwin, and the Duke of Wellington. The Rt. Honble. Lady Eleanor Butler and Miss Ponsonby, *lithograph, after 1831.*
PFORZHEIMER COLLECTION

The other great pleasure of their lives was home improvement, and over their many years together the ladies added to Plas Newydd constantly; it had become a small mansion with a farm by the time Eleanor Butler died in 1829. (Sarah Ponsonby, though sixteen years younger, followed her in 1831.) Because of this impulse to improve – it was a rage they shared with many others in rural Britain – the ladies were chronically in debt. However, although owing money sent many into debtors' exile across the Channel, Ponsonby and Butler, unlike Harriette Wilson or Dora Jordan, did not die alone in France. In fact, they managed their money troubles adroitly in Wales. They were able to live, indeed, exactly as they had planned when they eloped, in loving and intimate friendship away from the world.

The world often came to visit them, however: William Wordsworth, Sir Walter Scott, the writer Mme de Genlis, the scientist Sir Humphry Davy, a young Charles Darwin, and the Duke of Wellington, among many others, came to the cottage over the years. It became a tourist attraction, as visitors came to see the cottage and enjoy the placid life and devoted affection the ladies shared. Sarah Ponsonby, Eleanor Butler, and their way of life had a charisma that is gone now, the victim of a wider acceptance of lesbian ways of life.

Do we, then, know that they were lesbians? There is no direct evidence. If they had flaunted sexual passion for each other, they would quickly have been run out of Llangollen. When a newspaper report did insinuate that they were lesbians, the ladies were insulted and wounded. Yet the rumors persisted, as they do even now. Hester Thrale Piozzi, Samuel Johnson's friend and patron, who moved to Northern Wales in her late middle age, was also a good friend of the ladies and yet described them as "damned Sapphists" in her diary. This has been rightly described as an "example of the doublethink that made it possible to be aware of lesbian possibilities, yet defend romantic friendship as the epitome of moral purity."[29] But what is being suppressed by this double consciousness? Perhaps it's the same thing that was suppressed when gambling and adultery became unacceptable among women of the very highest classes: gaiety in the original use of the word. While there were no fewer ways for women to get into trouble in the Victorian period, they carried a heavier moral burden, as they pursued their pleasures with straight faces. If they had flaunted sexual passion for each other, they would quickly have been run out of Llangollen. When a newspaper report did insinuate that they were lesbians, the ladies were insulted and wounded. Yet the rumors persisted, as they do even now. Hester Thrale Piozzi, Samuel Johnson's friend and patron, who moved to Northern Wales in her late middle age, was also a good friend of the ladies and yet described them as "damned Sapphists" in her diary. This has been rightly described as an "example of the doublethink that made it possible to be aware of lesbian possibilities, yet defend romantic friendship as the epitome of moral purity."[29] But what is being suppressed by this double consciousness? Perhaps it's the same thing that was suppressed when gambling and adultery became unacceptable among women of the very highest classes: gaiety in the original use of the word. While there were no fewer ways for women to get into trouble in the Victorian period, they carried a heavier moral burden, as they pursued their pleasures with straight faces.

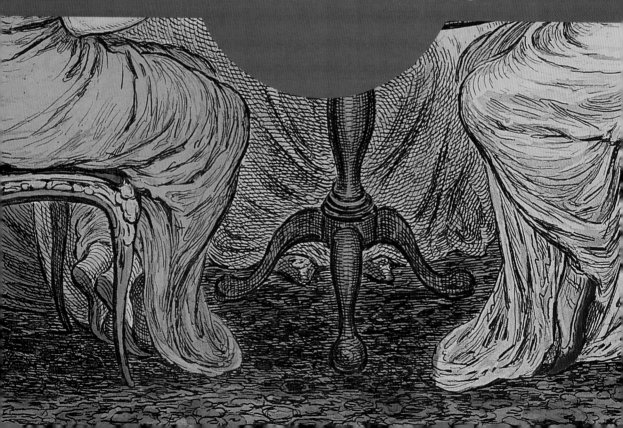

Chapter Five

STRONGER PASSIONS OF THE MIND:
WOMEN IN LITERATURE
AND THE VISUAL ARTS

OPPORTUNITIES FOR ENJOYING SIN may have grown scarcer over the Romantic period, but it was an enormously fruitful time for female readers and writers. Without pretending to be a history of women writers of the time, this chapter will present some of its most prominent figures. Their legacy is mixed in quality: while some novels of the period are classics, and many are still read for pleasure, the enormous quantity of poetry that women published, much of it written in heroic haste to support families, is now largely forgotten. The chapter ends with a complement of visual artists, fewer in number than writers, but among whom there are characters and works worth remembering.

WOMEN READING AND WRITING IN THE ROMANTIC PERIOD

A brief overview of the state of readers and writers in Romantic-era Britain will clarify some reasons for women's success in the literary marketplace. The audience for leisure reading grew quickly toward the end of the eighteenth century. Literacy rates rose, partly because – as we have seen in the efforts of Hannah More – elementary education was being extended to more children. The critical mass of readers needed to support a popular press had been firmly established by the end of the eighteenth century, and both newspapers and literary periodicals reviewed books of all kinds. Improved transportation carried books to places where they had formerly been scarce, and while London was the center of publishing, Dublin and Edinburgh had flourishing trades as well, and there were publishers to be found in most of the major provincial cities.

Many books found multiple readers, since reading aloud, both at home and in public places such as taverns and coffee houses, was far commoner than it is now. Literacy, though rising, was still far from universal, but almost everyone could listen. In addition, public readings by actors were popular entertainments; Sarah Siddons ended her career by giving celebrated readings in Shakespeare. The practice had a particular significance for women, who spent long hours in sewing, no matter what their social class – so many, indeed, that when women write of "my work" in letters, they usually refer to needlework – and these times were far more pleasant if someone read to the rest of the group.

The other means by which a book might have multiple users was the circulating library – a term that carried very different connotations in the Romantic era than it now has. Circulating libraries, which were entirely commercial enterprises, ran by subscription – a guinea (one pound plus a shilling) per quarter was a common charge for the fashionable libraries. Naturally, they provided books: history, poetry, essays, sermons, conduct books, and, above all, novels. Far from being quiet places for study, however, circulating libraries were

In search of ...

This young woman, coyly identified in the title of this 1782 mezzotint as a "Beauty in Search of Knowledge," is about to enter a circulating library. These commercial establishments provided more than just books – they were places to meet friends and flirt with strangers. PFORZHEIMER COLLECTION

places to meet and socialize, and while they were patronized by both sexes, they had a feminine air. Many sold stationery, pens, penknives, wafers, sealing wax, and other writing accessories; they might also sell sheet music, jewelry, snuffboxes, ribbons, and other small luxury items.

In this literary atmosphere, a number of elements enabled women to flourish as writers. Writing occupied a space between the public and the private spheres: while there has long been a sense that women were prohibited from writing, or that it was thought "improper," this was far from being always the case. A woman (or a man, for that matter) might sign her work or remain anonymous, depending on her circumstances and character; a writer who published a successful work anonymously could always use "by the author of ..." for her next one, to maintain and build her readership. For genteel women who found unexpectedly that they needed to earn money, writing was an ideal – and almost the only – option. It was cheap in itself, requiring no capital and little in the way of tools; it could be done at home, in secret if need be; and it required no training, except the reading they would have been doing for years for their own amusement or learning.

POETS

Many women turned naturally to novels, a newer form that had become very popular with readers and, for some practitioners, quite lucrative. But at the end of the eighteenth century, poetry was still the genre with the most prestige, and was read far more often than it is now. A poet, unlike a novelist, did not have to apologize for what she was doing. Many works that would now be written in prose were then in verse: Erasmus Darwin's *Loves of the Plants* (1792; the original 1791 edition had the less attractive title *The Botanic Garden*), for example, a botanical study of plant reproduction by Charles Darwin's grandfather, was written in couplets.

Perhaps the most significant feature of the poets of the Romantic era is that they were enormously different from each other. The sardonic and witty stanzas of George Gordon Byron, Lord Byron's *Don Juan* could hardly be more different from the fourteen-syllable lines of William Blake's majestic and mysterious *Jerusalem* if one had actually been writing in Latin and the other in Hebrew. Even between poets who were great friends with and influences on each other, such as Wordsworth and Coleridge, there are wide differences in style and subjects.

A few generalizations about poetic styles in the period may be made, however. Many poets, male and female, chose simpler styles than the syntactically complex ones that the previous generation had employed, since they no longer looked back to Greece and Rome as the primary models for poetry. And this break was conscious: Romantic poets did not call themselves Romantic, but they were well aware that they were renovating poetic tradition, and announced the fact in documents such as Wordsworth's famous Preface to the second edition of *Lyrical Ballads*, where he calls for poetry that speaks the language of ordinary men. The Napoleonic Wars touched literature as well as everything else, and expressions of patriotic feeling became frequent. Shakespeare's reputation as a native-born English poet and playwright with little classical education rose sharply at the end of the eighteenth century. Ballads and poetry that recalled British history were also turned to patriotic purposes and became extremely popular, and English audiences gained a new appreciation of the literary heritages of Ireland, Wales, and Scotland, all now subsumed after 1800, willingly or not, under the new name "United Kingdom."

Felicia Hemans (1793–1835)

Many of these general features can be seen in the work of Felicia Hemans, who competed closely with Byron for the title of bestselling poet of her generation. She was born to a loving Anglican family, and raised in Wales. Felicia Browne, as she was then, distinguished herself from her peers by her talent for languages, learning French, Spanish, Italian, Portuguese, Latin, and German. And her success was nearly instant. Her first book of poems, appearing when she was fourteen, had no fewer than nine hundred subscribers, among them Percy Bysshe Shelley, only a year older than she. Her marriage lasted about six years and produced five children, all of them boys. At that point her husband, a Captain Alfred Hemans, deserted her; unlike Caroline Norton's husband, he left his wife to enjoy the profits of her work in peace.

These were considerable. The sole breadwinner for the family, Hemans owed her success to prolific publishing, a keen ear, a sensitive heart, and a completely conventional morality. Her poetry often describes domestic scenes – one volume is entitled *The Domestic Affections*, and one of her best-known lyrics, the 1827 "Homes of England," praises, in successive stanzas, "the stately homes of England," the "merry homes," the "blessed homes," the "cottage homes," and so on, ending with "the free, fair, homes of England." By 1827, the ruinous Napoleonic Wars were long over; Britain had an empire and the strongest navy in the world, and poetry like Mrs. Hemans's fed a strong appetite for sentimental patriotism and its domestic counterpart, the love of one's home.

While she did not support feminist ideas, Hemans was strongly conscious of herself as a *woman* writer, at home in the realm of femininity, which she idealized as she did England. Her most popular volume, *Records of Woman*, told stories of women around the world and across time, taking in Greece, Rome,

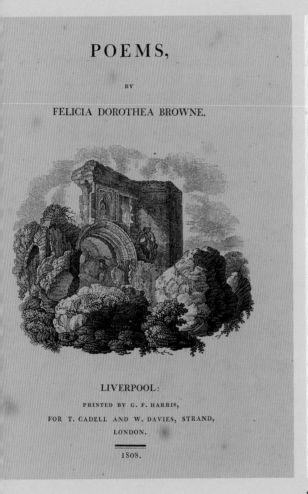

POEMS,

BY

FELICIA DOROTHEA BROWNE.

LIVERPOOL:

PRINTED BY G. F. HARRIS,

FOR T. CADELL AND W. DAVIES, STRAND,

LONDON.

1808.

Printed by W. E. West.   Engraved by W. Holl.

Felicia Hemans

Instant success

Felicia Hemans, one of the bestselling poets of her generation, fed an appetite for sentimental patriotism and love of home. Her first book, simply titled Poems, *appeared in 1808, when she was fourteen, and had no fewer than nine hundred subscribers, among them Percy Bysshe Shelley. Her work was the sole support of her five sons, and later portraits, such as this 1837 engraving by W. Holl, after W. E. West, show a confident benignity.* PFORZHEIMER COLLECTION

Italy, North America, and ancient Carthage. Sex and sentiment, thus, trump geography and history as a way of experiencing the world: readers could feel at home in her poems because they conveyed strong and familiar emotions. The poetic tale of an American Indian woman, despairing because her husband has deserted her, who steers a canoe bearing herself and her children over a waterfall, is typical of Hemans's emotional palette. Byron was scornful, saying, for instance, that it was obvious that she had never been to Greece. This was true; being the single responsible parent to five young children makes travel difficult. It is also true that there is a synthetic quality to Hemans's settings: they are made up from guidebooks. But if Byron had wit where Hemans had pathos, they both had an extraordinary sense for what audiences wanted to read; and while Byron's early poetry made his readers want to run off to the Levant to take up with corsairs, Hemans made them feel that there was equal value in being an Englishwoman in an English home.

Letitia Elizabeth Landon (1802–1835)

In some ways, Letitia Elizabeth Landon had a great deal in common with Felicia Hemans. Like Hemans, she wrote to support her children; like Hemans, she enjoyed early fame and great popular success; like Hemans, she died young. Unlike Hemans, Letitia Elizabeth Landon bore her three children out of wedlock. She found much of her writing material in her secret relationship with the father of her children and editor of her poetry, William Jerdan, twenty years her senior and married to another woman. What is extraordinary about Landon is not that she lived a double life, but that she got away with it for so long. Evidence that Landon was a single mother surfaced only in the early twenty-first century, and while it may not revive her reputation as a poet, it has certainly transformed it.[1]

The facts of her life are brief: born and educated in London, she began writing as a young girl. When some of her poems came to the attention of William Jerdan, editor of the popular *Literary Gazette*, he took her under his wing, instructing her in the writing of poetry, taking her to exhibitions of paintings and the theater. Either he or she would usually write a review of what they had seen, and the result was that, like Wollstonecraft before her, Landon's first experience of the professional writing life was as a journalist.[2] Poetry, however, remained her first passion, and eros itself was from the beginning her subject. This was possible only because she was "protected by the supposition of her sexual innocence."[3] Her love for Jerdan was, apparently, a good deal stronger than his for her – indeed, she seems to have pursued him – and she continued the affair not just for the sake of love but for that of poetry as well, simply so that she would have material from which to write.[4]

Landon and Jerdan were lovers from a few years after they became acquainted into the 1830s. Even the three children she had by him did not entirely reveal the relationship to the public. When the rumors finally became too much to deny, she accepted the marriage proposal of a near-stranger and moved to what is now Ghana, where her new husband held a colonial position. She was found mysteriously dead only a few months after her marriage, with a bottle of prussic acid in her hand. Her marriage was not entirely happy, and the automatic speculation, of course, is suicide; but Landon was in the habit of taking small doses of prussic acid for her health, and had recently written cheerful letters home, planning for the future. Her death remains mysterious.

Byron famously writes in *Don Juan*, his dizzying picaresque epic: "Man's love is of his life a thing apart, / 'Tis woman's whole existence ..."[5] Letitia Landon's extraordinary life both contradicts him and proves him correct: her love for Jerdan was kept wholly apart from the rest of her world; her love for poetry gave form to her whole existence.

Poet of eros
The poet Letitia Landon, shown here in an anonymous etching and engraving, took eros as her great subject, finding much of her material in her secret relationship with the editor of her poetry and the father of her children, who was also twenty years her senior and married to another woman. PRINT COLLECTION

PLAYWRIGHTS

In the Romantic period, theater was hugely popular, and attended by all social classes in London, Dublin, Edinburgh, and at the provincial theaters. The lion's share of glamour, however, belonged to the actors: David Garrick, Sarah Siddons, and her brother John Philip Kemble were stars, adored, spied on, and publicized in a way that had not been possible before the advent of a thriving newspaper industry. Playwrights were, on the whole, underpaid and rarely depended solely on the theater for their livelihood. Still, a hit led to both fame and fortune; a play that had a good run (ten nights or more) could be considerably more lucrative than a novel. For women who loved theater but wanted to preserve their reputations, playwriting was safer than acting, although it still required meticulous care and constant mention by the chaste playwright to her friends and acquaintances that she was, indeed, a respectable woman.

Joanna Baillie Of the living playwrights who mattered most to Romantic
(1762–1851) audiences, two were women, and Joanna Baillie is
still remembered as an innovator in the psychological
development of theatrical character. Baillie came from
a Scottish family, headed by a stern and emotionally ungenerous Presbyterian
minister who neglected his daughter's education. On his death, her maternal
uncle William Hunter, a brilliant physician and medical researcher, took in the
family; when he died in 1783, Baillie, her sister, and her mother moved to London
where her brother, Matthew, was establishing a medical reputation of his own.
Her life in London was devoted to her aging mother.

With this sort of background, a life in the theater seems unlikely, and
Baillie in fact began as a poet. The ambition to write plays seems to have struck
suddenly: "It was whilst imprisoned by the heat of a summer afternoon, and
seated by her mother's side engaged in needlework, that the thought of essaying
dramatic work burst upon her."[6] In 1798 Baillie began publishing her *Series of
plays in which it is attempted to delineate the stronger passions of the mind, each
passion being the subject of a tragedy and a comedy*. If one of the hallmarks of
modernity is the self-conscious examination of one's emotions, separately and
(as it were) dispassionately, the *Plays on the Passions*, as they were called, can
be noted as a genuine innovation. They aroused a great deal of interest, and were
an immediate success, partly for their subject and partly for Baillie's use of more
natural dialogue than had been customary in tragedy. Published anonymously,
they left many playing what must have been a favorite parlor amusement of the
time, guessing at the author's identity. Readers were unsure even of the author's
gender. Hester Thrale Piozzi, Samuel Johnson's friend, got it right: she was sure
they had been written by a woman, since they featured middle-aged female
protagonists – and, she said, "a man has no notion of mentioning a woman after
she is five and twenty."[7]

In 1800 Sarah Siddons and her brother John Philip Kemble acted in the
first production of Baillie's *De Monfort*, a tragedy based on the life of the medieval
English baron Simon de Montfort, and illustrating hatred. Later performances
did reasonably well, but this first showing was not a theatrical success: audiences
were, quite simply, bored. Readers may feel passions conveyed in words, but
audiences require action. Baillie's writing was better than her instinct for
staging, and her refusal to attend rehearsals meant that she lost the opportunity
playwrights had then and now to make revisions.[8] The refusal was born at least
partly from her wish to preserve her reputation, though even at the time her
concern was slightly excessive.

Off stage, Baillie kept her passions to herself, and never married. And
celibacy was the price demanded of unmarried women for a mind entirely free
from worries about one's reputation. One contemporary wrote of her: "It was

Passions of the mind

Joanna Baillie wrote a popular series of dramas that concentrated on single emotions, known as Plays of the Passions. *The tragedy* De Monfort, *illustrating hatred, was based on the life of the medieval English baron Simon de Montfort.* Alterations of the Tragedy of De Monfort, *autograph manuscript, unsigned, undated [1817 watermark].* BERG COLLECTION

difficult to persuade yourself that the little, insignificant, and rather commonplace-looking individual before you could have conceived and embodied with such potent energy, the deadly hatred of De Monfort or the fiery love of Basil."[9] While giving up the physical expression of sexuality is, undoubtedly, a sacrifice, it would be presumptuous to say now how much of a sacrifice it was for Joanna Baillie. Her career illustrates, at least, that propriety by no means entailed giving up a life dedicated to passion.

Elizabeth Inchbald (1753–1821)

Elizabeth Inchbald made the same sacrifice as Joanna Baillie and lived as a famously chaste woman after widowhood at twenty-six in 1779. Unlike Joanna Baillie, she spent her life in the theater as an actress, translator, critic, editor, and playwright. She wrote one memorable novel, *A Simple Story* (1791), and the slighter *Nature and Art* (1796). Inchbald married an actor and began her career in the provin-cial theater, as her friend Sarah Siddons had, but unlike Siddons she had only moderate success on the stage. She began writing for the theater in the 1780s and was productive in one form or another into the 1810s, spending many of those years on plays for Covent Garden. She was renowned for her beauty and intelligence, and notorious for her frugality; one friend, on being invited to tea, asked if he should bring his own bun.

Because she was so thoroughly immersed in the theatrical world, Elizabeth Inchbald found propriety a more difficult proposition than Joanna Baillie did. Her life illustrates the painful lengths to which women with public lives might go to maintain a spotless reputation. When Inchbald realized that her friend Mary Wollstonecraft could not have been married to Gilbert Imlay, since she had just announced herself to be the new wife of William Godwin – also a friend – Inchbald refused to go to the theater with them as they had arranged. She did not wish to be seen with a woman who had borne a child out of wedlock, as Wollstonecraft had to Imlay. Wollstonecraft was deeply injured, but Inchbald insisted to Godwin on her rectitude even soon after Wollstonecraft's death in childbirth.

Yet her politics were not those of Hannah More; on paper, they were close to Godwin's and Wollstonecraft's. She believed, as they did, that the injustice of the British government was systemic and deserved protest. And she did so in her plays: *I'll Tell You What* (1785) questions the marriage laws; *Such Things Are* (1787) decries the gruesome conditions in British prisons. Most famously, *Lovers' Vows* (1798), Inchbald's adaptation from August Kotzebue's German, depicts a couple who bear a child out of wedlock and are, at the end, after twenty years of separation, allowed to marry and live happily ever after. Today it is

An independent woman

Elizabeth Inchbald spent her life in the theater as an actress, translator, critic, editor, and playwright. Renowned for her beauty and intelligence, she became a target of satire because of her radical politics and her independent (though celibate) life after being widowed at twenty-six. In I'll Tell You What! *(the title of one of her plays), Henry Wigstead caricatures her as living in squalor, with a bottle of gin and a volume of the Earl of Rochester's erotic poetry on the table. This portrait, by contrast, presents its subject as a paragon of propriety. Henry Wigstead,* I'll Tell You What!, *lithograph, 1790s.* PRINT COLLECTION; *Frontispiece portrait from James Boaden,* Memoirs of Mrs. Inchbald *(London, 1833).* PFORZHEIMER COLLECTION

remembered largely because in Jane Austen's 1814 novel, *Mansfield Park*, the Bertram family, stricken with the fever for amateur theatricals, prepare to stage the play. The emotions generated during rehearsals lead directly to an elopement between one pair of characters and the breakup of a marriage between another. Inchbald herself defended the play by arguing that the unmarried mother's suffering through twenty years of solitude and poverty more than atoned for her sins. And unlike Joanna Baillie, Inchbald was knowledgeable about staging and knew that in performance, audiences felt the unmarried mother's remorse.[10]

In any case, her own reputation, although spotless, was also vulnerable, simply because she was a woman living independently in late eighteenth-century Britain, and therefore a fair target. The caricature on page 101 shows Inchbald as she emphatically was not: besotted with gin, living in squalor with the journalistic instruments for puffing – i.e., promoting by stealth – her own works all around her, a volume of the Earl of Rochester's very suggestive poetry on the table. Despite its unkindness, there is something rather cozy about the scene and even, perhaps, something rather accurate: what's emphasized by its untidiness is Inchbald's solitude. This in fact was the most extraordinary thing about her. While many successful women writers of the period were widowed or single, most of these did not live alone: the age could bear a woman unattached to a man, but for a well-known, reputable woman to live entirely on her own was unusual and required courage. Elizabeth Inchbald was deeply uncharitable in cutting her friend; however, in doing so, she was not just commenting on what she perceived as Wollstonecraft's immoral behavior, but protecting her own independence of movement.

NOVEL WRITERS AND NOVEL READERS

The same sexual ethics had tainted the novel's reputation, which improved during the Romantic period – although, like a courtesan who has decided to go over to the side of propriety, it had a long way to go. Early on, novels were widely believed to be immoral, and to instruct young ladies in vice. It was customary to scoff at them: Jane Austen, in *Northanger Abbey* (1798; not published until 1818), describes the "common cant," imagining some hypothetical young lady's reply to being asked what she is reading: "'Only a novel!' ... only Cecilia, or Camilla, or Belinda." Austen rebuts: "only, in short, some work in which the greatest powers of the mind are displayed, in which the most thorough knowledge of human nature ... the liveliest effusion of wit and humour, are conveyed to the world in the best chosen language."[11] Jane Austen's mockery indicates that by 1798 the battle for respectability had been largely won, although disapproval continued in some families far into the nineteenth century.

Some reasons for antipathy to the novel also explain why it quickly became associated with women readers and writers. First, it was entirely possible for women with even the most limited education to write novels, while they were barred from other genres – sermons, for instance – because they were barred from their associated professions. Second, novels allowed women to imagine themselves in situations more gratifying or more exciting than, or simply different from, those in which they lived. This is not to say that novels are only escapist fantasy, but they sometimes serve this function for both readers and writers. Third, while novels might employ everything one knows of human nature, they also tend to be highly formulaic, and for women who were writing for money, this was a useful truth. The tossed-off "only a novel" meant that the artistic stakes were as low or as high as one set them for oneself. While women writing novels in the Romantic period entered a tradition with some very honorable exemplars in the works of Miguel de Cervantes, Henry Fielding, Samuel Richardson, and Laurence Sterne, they could also look for models to the ephemeral, overweight, three-volume tales they found at their town's circulating library.

Frances Burney (1752–1840)

Alternatively, of course, a woman could aim to equal the masters. Jane Austen's "only a Cecilia" is a direct compliment to Frances Burney's second novel, *Cecilia, or Memoirs of an Heiress* (1782). (The name "Fanny," still a familiar way of speaking about her, was used only in her family circle.) Her first, *Evelina, or a Young Lady's Entrance into the World* (1778), was written and published in secret, only acknowledged after it had won enthusiastic praise from the lexicographer Samuel Johnson and Hester Thrale (later Piozzi), both friends of Charles Burney, the novelist's father, an eminent and ambitious musicologist, composer, and performer. *Evelina* tells through letters the story of a young woman's introduction to London's theater, balls, pleasure gardens, and social codes, ending with the discovery of her parentage and marriage to her true love. This narrative reflects social as well as literary convention. Young women did enter the world through the London social season, and if all went according to plan, a woman's independence in both novels and the material world lasted only for the months, or few years at most, between her being introduced into society and her marriage.

Evelina's interest comes from Burney's simultaneous presentation of different points of view as she manages the tensions of an epistolary novel: while the heroine, in her letters, describes the tortures of social embarrassment and displays her growing wisdom, the author skewers the vulgar family into which Evelina has been introduced. Burney herself knew both the social agony – she

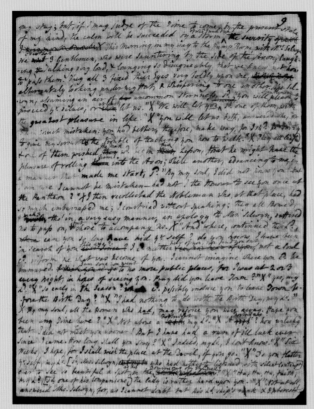

*Frances Burney's first
novel,* Evelina, or a Young
Lady's Entrance into the
World *(1778), was pub-
lished anonymously, and
acknowledged by its
author only after it had
won enthusiastic praise. It
narrates a young woman's
introduction to London
society and her eventual
triumph in love.* Evelina,
*autograph manuscript,
unsigned, undated [ca.
1778].* BERG COLLECTION

A novelist's parlor

*Many women made a living
by their pens, and this inviting
parlor shows what the rewards
of a successful career might be.
It belonged to the Irish writer
Lady Sydney Morgan (1783–
1859), best known for her 1807
novel* The Wild Irish Girl. *For
much of her life she was also
renowned as a hostess, and
her parlor was an important
and sought-after Dublin social
destination. Frontispiece from*
Lady Sydney Morgan, Passages
from My Autobiography
(London, 1859). PFORZHEIMER
COLLECTION

was painfully shy and remained so for years – and the courage she gives Evelina at moments of greatest need.

Burney's career and her novels are marked by integrity and inhibition. At fifteen she made a bonfire of everything she had written. But she could not entirely betray her powerful creative drive, and when she found herself preoccupied with thoughts of a sequel to one of the burnt novels, she returned to writing. With help from her brother, Burney published *Evelina* anonymously. The success of the book and its successor, *Cecilia*, led indirectly to her appointment as the second keeper of the robes to Queen Charlotte, the wife of George III, a job which she found little less than torture in its restrictions on her time and movements. Here was propriety in its most imprisoning form. She took the position only to please Charles Burney, and was freed from it after five years, as her health was imperiled by the tedium.

Meanwhile, Burney had been working constantly at her diary, her other important contribution to British literature. She portrayed in careful detail scenes like the one in which she was chased around Kew Gardens by George III, whom she believed to be insane, although he had, on this occasion, recently recovered. After leaving the court, Burney was able to live more for her own sake, and she married, with her father's reluctant consent, a genteel but impecunious French refugee from the Revolution. When the Napoleonic Wars stranded them on the Continent for more than ten years, Burney continued to record her experiences, including the Battle of Waterloo and a mastectomy performed (as all operations then were) without anaesthesia. She survived into Victoria's reign, outliving her husband, her only son, and her father, whose memoirs she edited. Burney's later novels do not equal *Evelina* in wit, but their concerns deepen. The heroine of her last, *The Wanderer, or Female Troubles* (1814), comes close to starvation as she learns that central truth of life in the Romantic era, that there were very few jobs for genteel ladies. She is given a wedding at the end, but *The Wanderer* is the novel of a writer who has undergone both acute suffering and the tedium of a long life.

Maria Edgeworth (1767–1849)

Maria Edgeworth's life was dominated by her father, Richard Lovell Edgeworth, to an even greater degree than Frances Burney's was by hers: she never married and spent most of her life at the family estate in Edgeworthstown, in County Longford, Ireland. While Burney was, at times, palpably held back by Charles Burney, Richard Edgeworth helped to launch his daughter's career, and collaborated with her in her pedagogical work – which had its roots in his own. The family interest in teaching young children was fueled by Richard's prolific paternity:

Pleasures and horrors of reading

James Gillray's Tales of Wonder! *(1802)
clings to the old belief that novels were
dangerous objects – especially the extremely
popular Gothic novels, and most especially
Matthew Gregory Lewis's highly improper*
The Monk *(1796), with its supernatural
and sexual elements and a finale featuring
the Devil himself. Gillray shows women
thoroughly enjoying the frissons of horror
it delivered.* PRINT COLLECTION

married four times, he fathered twenty-two children altogether. Maria, his eldest daughter by his first marriage, acted as surrogate mother to many of her siblings and half-siblings. Her life was defined by being a lovingly dutiful daughter.

Maria Edgeworth's strength is her astonishing variety of subjects. Her world was enlarged by her father's very wide range of interests, which included science, industry, politics, and agriculture as well as education. For parents and teachers, she wrote (with the help of her father and a few other Edgeworths) works on progressive pedagogy, such as *Practical Education* and *The Parents' Assistant*. On her own, she supported serious education for women with *Letters to Literary Ladies*. For poor readers, there was the straightforward condescension of the *Moral Tales*. For genteel audiences, there was the more sophisticated but highly moralistic *Fashionable Tales*. For the Anglo-Irish who found the native Catholic population unnerving with their foreign language, foreign religion, and continual political uprisings, there was the "Essay on Irish Bulls," showing that the Irish were amiable, half-witted countryfolk. For the same audience, *Castle Rackrent* and *The Absentee* portrayed the Irish as anything but half-wits, and showed that the Anglo-Irish had brought at least some of their troubles on themselves by their gouging rents and callous treatment of their tenants. Finally, for twenty-first-century audiences, there is *Belinda*, now Edgeworth's most enjoyable novel, one that still surprises, with female duels, interracial marriage, characters worried about breast cancer, the whole tied together by the love of a rational young woman for a rational young man.

Edgeworth's missing audience, of course, is the Irish Catholics themselves, for whom she wrote no major works. Her social position as an Anglo-Irish landlord may have prevented her from fully sympathizing with her tenants, although she supported endeavors such as a school founded by one of her brothers to teach children of "all religious persuasions" (i.e., Catholic, Anglican, and Dissenting) together. A significant incident from her life shows an ability to appreciate other cultures that makes one wonder if things might not have been different. Edgeworth's 1812 novel *The Absentee* is casually anti-Semitic in a way that was common in the nineteenth century, making its only prominent Jewish character a villain. When, in 1815, a young American named Rachel Mordecai – who by chance had the same last name as the character in question – wrote to Edgeworth, taking her gently to task for the portrayal, she promptly made amends by including episodes in her next novel, *Harrington* (1817), in which characters are taught that anti-Semitism is an outdated prejudice.[12] Edgeworth's reaction is, perhaps, slightly facile, but her readiness and ability to rethink her views are the secret of her strength as a novelist: while her moral sensibility is exemplary of the conventions of her time, place, religion, and social position, her extraordinary imagination is far more powerful and supple.

Jane Austen
(1775–1817)

The characters of Jane Austen's novels are almost uniformly conventional, as her own life appears to have been. She was born the daughter of a vicar in Hampshire, and grew up there, moving to the spa town of Bath, and finally to Chawton, also in Hampshire. Although Austen did not travel abroad, she was no country mouse; she was familiar with London and its theaters from numerous visits, and knew Bath intimately, from both her own health troubles and those of her family. Her closest friend was her sister Cassandra, to whom the letter reproduced here was written. Neither she nor Cassandra ever married, and the sisters lived with their family, plying the occupations of old maids: needlework, caring for nieces and nephews, visiting, playing cards, writing letters, and – in Jane Austen's case – polishing masterpieces of prose fiction.

Jane Austen's world, in short, consisted of provincial England and its gentry, and her novels are confined to these places and their people. Why, when she was working in such limited circumstances, with such a tiny palette, has she – alone of the writers in this book – become a major figure in world literature? By her own reckoning, her strength came from the limitations themselves. Austen knew her strength and the materials her imagination required to work well, writing to her niece, Anna, who was working on a novel of her own: "You are now collecting your People delightfully, getting them into exactly such a spot as is the delight of my life; – 3 or 4 families in a Country Village is the very thing to work on."¹⁵ In every one of her six finished novels – *Northanger Abbey*, *Pride and Prejudice*, *Sense and Sensibility*, *Mansfield Park*, *Emma*, and *Persuasion* – the heroine marries the man she ought to, but for Austen dramas are ethical, not merely conjugal. The same could be said for Hannah More, but where More's single interest is the morals, Austen's vision is multiple, as she develops the moral, social, economic, and intellectual lives of her characters. And where More is humorless, the hallmark of Austen's novels is their fine wit. (She is capable of being outright funny as well, especially in her juvenilia.) But it is not humor alone that attaches readers so strongly to Austen's novels. Employing a technique known, rather awkwardly, as free indirect discourse, Austen moves in and out of her heroine's mind within a single sentence, so that the problems with which the heroine is grappling belong simultaneously to her and to the reader, while the narrator maintains an ironic distance. The effect is rather like listening to chamber music and playing the first violin part at the same time: one is *both* participant and audience in a Jane Austen novel.

The double effect inspires considerable emulation. Members of the Jane Austen Society of North America, for instance, write sequels to the novels, maintain a website known as the World of Pemberley (named for the estate owned by Fitzwilliam Darcy, Elizabeth Bennet's successful suitor in *Pride and Prejudice*), and have been known to dress in Regency costume and dance at

The world on a two-inch bit of ivory

Jane Austen's six masterpieces of fiction work on a small scale – she spoke of her novels as paintings on "a little bit of ivory two inches wide." Their artistry, however, is beloved and studied everywhere. An unmarried woman living a quiet but full life in the English provinces, Austen wrote this letter, full of the alert social observation so typical of her novels, to her closest friend, her sister Cassandra, who painted almost the only known portrait of the writer. Jane Austen, *stipple engraving, after a watercolor by Cassandra Austen,* 1870. PRINT COLLECTION; Jane Austen, *autograph letter, signed, November 28,* 1815. BERG COLLECTION

[autograph letter in Jane Austen's hand]

Hans Place. Sunday Nov: 26.

My Dearest

The Parcel arrived safely, & I am much obliged to you for your trouble...

cotillions with other Austen fans. There is good artistic reason for this degree of affection: Jane Austen gives one a sense of life, funnier, better balanced, and better written than one knows it. She died, probably of Addison's disease, in 1817 and was buried in Winchester Cathedral. Only in the first half of the twentieth century was she universally acknowledged a major writer. If her own life was not, in its events, extraordinary, her afterlife has been nothing less.

Ann Radcliffe (1764–1823)

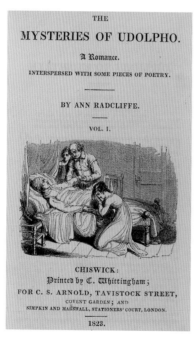

Safely sublime

Ann Radcliffe always furnished a rational explanation for the mysteries in her Gothic cliff-hangers. In The Mysteries of Udolpho *(1797, shown here in an 1823 edition from Chiswick) and other novels, Radcliffe also uses landscape – sublime mountains, luxuriantly green valleys, and ruined Gothic castles visited only by shepherds – to give outward expression to her characters' feelings.*

PFORZHEIMER COLLECTION

If Jane Austen's life seems quiet, Ann Radcliffe's by comparison is nearly silent. When the nineteenth-century poet Christina Rossetti considered writing a biography of her, she gave up for lack of materials. More has been discovered since then, but the most important documents we have of Radcliffe's are still her three major novels, *The Romance of the Forest* (1791), *The Italian* (1794), and *The Mysteries of Udolpho* (1797), vastly popular in their day and for decades afterward. Although many readers now lack the patience for her leisurely syntax and descriptions of landscape, the novels retain a power as the forbears of our own darker interests: she is the master of the frightening implication.

Mrs. Radcliffe, as readers called her, was born Ann Ward, in London to a family in trade with a Unitarian background. They moved later to Bath, where her father sold Josiah Wedgwood's china. Her marriage to William Radcliffe, a newspaper publisher, was apparently happy. She wrote her single work of nonfiction, a volume of travels in Germany and Holland, in partial collaboration with him, and retired at the height of her fame, achieving an impenetrable obscurity. Radcliffe's propriety was unassailable, although her persistent, willful invisibility was unbearable to journalists, who invented or embroidered rumors that she had been incarcerated in a madhouse. She may, according to her most recent biographer, have suffered in later years from depression, but her end came, prosaically and painfully, from asthma.[14]

While Jane Austen turned for her material to the society she knew, Ann Radcliffe moved in precisely the opposite direction, and set her novels in countries she had never visited. This may have been an advantage, for Radcliffe has no interest in the drama of the interior life. Where Jane Austen draws the reader into the lives of her characters, Radcliffe uses landscape to give outward expression to her characters' feelings. While her novels are ostensibly mysteries, using a standard cast of handsome hero, beautiful heroine, and craggy-faced villain, with appearances by dying fathers and long-lost mothers, their real protagonists are the landscapes. They are based on those of her favorite painters, Claude Lorrain and Salvator Rosa, the one French, the other Italian, seventeenth-century artists who specialized in sublime mountains, luxuriantly green valleys, and ruined Gothic castles visited only by shepherds. Radcliffe studied her geographies and guidebooks carefully, as well as the paintings, and what her characters lack in particularity is given to the descriptions of their endless travels from castle to monastery to ancient house. Readers loved both her leisurely evocations of the sublime and picturesque and her equally leisurely mysteries, which, on religious principle, were always rationally explained. The demands of propriety may not have prevented women from getting away from home; but they did make it difficult to get away from self-consciousness, and Radcliffe's scenery provided, for many readers, a holiday from the restrictive contours of reality.

Mary Shelley (1797–1851)

For Mary Shelley, the Alps were no fantasy. She had seen them on her stolen honeymoon with Percy Bysshe Shelley, and her imagination had to venture further than Ann Radcliffe's had in its search for the sublime. No work discussed here has had as much ink spilt and film shot over it as *Frankenstein, or the Modern Prometheus* (1818), already discussed briefly in Chapter One, and the story of its creation is itself now almost as famous as the novel.

At the time of *Frankenstein*'s conception, in June of 1816, Mary Wollstonecraft Godwin was eighteen. Two years earlier she had eloped with Shelley (still married to Harriet at the time); she had already twice given birth and mourned the death of her first child. During a summer ruined by constant rain and cold, the result of a volcanic eruption in Indonesia, they found themselves by Lake Geneva. Lord Byron, famous for his poetry and charisma, was their neighbor. A volume of German ghost stories, read aloud to pass the time, gave rise to a contest to write frightening stories of their own. Mary Godwin, encouraged to write something worthy of her parentage, searched for an idea, one that "would speak to the mysterious fears of our nature, and awaken thrilling horror," but for weeks found her mind barren.[15] After a night listening to Shelley and Byron discussing the possibility of reanimating the dead with electricity, the creature came to her in a dream, with "yellow, watery, but speculative eyes."[16] She began work on his novel the next morning.

In Mary Shelley's own time, *Frankenstein* became a popular play, the monster portrayed as an oversized man, displaying his origins as the "noble savage" of Enlightenment philosophy in his boldness, his bare chest, and his natural goodness. But the story of the young Swiss doctor and his problem child has had dozens of reincarnations and borne almost numberless interpretations. Shelley's novel supports them because its own origins are multiple, bringing together issues that have haunted its author and its readers: the joy and horror of motherhood; the relationship between science and the soul; the question of how and when life begins; the relationship between the artist and the work of art.

If *Frankenstein*'s hallmark is its multiple meanings, Mary Shelley's life was, after the death of her husband in a sailing accident off the Bay of Spezia in 1822, relatively monotonous. Her marriage, although fulfilling as few are, had not always been happy, and it was punctuated tragically by the deaths of her children (she gave birth to four, of whom only one son, Percy Florence, survived). Mary and Percy Bysshe Shelley spent about half of their life together in Italy, forming communities with a few friends both Italian and English. Among these, over the years, were Claire Clairmont, her own life scarred by the death at age four of Allegra, her illegitimate daughter by Byron; Margaret King Moore, Lady Mount Cashell, known to them all as Mrs. Mason; Prince Alexander Mavrocordato, active in the Greek fight for independence from Turkey; and Jane Williams, widowed when her husband died in the same accident that killed Shelley.

Mary Shelley returned to England two years after Shelley's drowning, still mourning. Although there were unconsummated entanglements in after-years – with both women and men – her emotional energies were largely dedicated to her son, her aging father, and her work. The last was made unnecessarily difficult by her husband's father, Sir Timothy Shelley. Embarrassed by his son's radical politics and sexually unorthodox life, he forced his daughter-in-law to agree, in return for a meager quarterly sum, to refrain from publishing Shelley's work or the biography she had planned to write. Thus, for reasons of propriety, the work that might have allowed Mary Shelley to move beyond grieving for her husband, that would have been useful to her finances and invaluable to scholars in the future, was lost. Godwin put it well – although in reference to other matters – when he remarked, "We live in squeamish days."[17]

Frankenstein's monster: Before Karloff

Frankenstein *was a popular stage play long before Boris Karloff appeared on movie screens with bolts in his neck. The actor Thomas P. Cooke, costumed in a Roman toga, made a career of the part, portraying a creature whose original, virtuous impulses are turned to the side of evil by human misunderstanding.* Mr. T. P. Cooke, of the Theatre Royal Covent Garden, *lithograph by N. Whittock, after Wagerman, ca. 1825.*
PFORZHEIMER COLLECTION

Birthplace of *Frankenstein*
This view of Lord Byron's residence on the shores of Lake Geneva shows where the famous ghost-story contest that gave rise to Mary Shelley's Frankenstein *took place. Lord Byron, Percy Bysshe Shelley, Mary Godwin (not yet married to Shelley), and their companions sought to entertain each other with stories; after weeks of frustration, the idea behind* Frankenstein *inspired her in a dream.* Diodati. The Residence of Lord Byron, *engraving by M. Osborne, after a drawing by W. Fursen, undated.* PFORZHEIMER COLLECTION

Despite the prohibition on memorializing her husband in print, Mary Shelley wrote almost continuously for much of the rest of her life to support Percy Florence. Shelley's oeuvre includes nearly all the popular genres of the period: she turned out novels, short stories for the gift annuals, volumes for a biographical encyclopedia, poetry, and travel books. The most memorable, and her most-read work today after *Frankenstein*, is *The Last Man* (1826), a futuristic tale in which a plague kills the inhabitants of the entire world, leaving a single survivor to tell his story; its characters bear transformed but legible resemblances to the friends and family Mary Shelley had lost.

CHILDREN'S WRITERS

The Romantic period also saw the maturing of a new mode of writing: the book for children. In fact, Mary Shelley's first publication was a work for children. When she was still a very small Mary Godwin, she contributed to an illustrated version of a song mocking a monolingual Englishman in France, who thinks that "Monsieur, je ne vous entends pas" ("Sir, I don't understand you") is the name of a great nobleman. Such songs were common during the Napoleonic Wars, but women's most important contributions to children's literature were their volumes of tales and their significant educational texts.

Mary Lamb (1764–1847) is hardly exemplary among the children's writers, but she is certainly extraordinary, and her contributions – the most enduringly popular of any of the period – will serve to show the best of what was produced then. Lamb's *Tales from Shakespear* (the final "e" was still optional), written with her brother Charles, have been in print continuously, or nearly so, since being published in 1807. With clear language and gentle humor, the twenty tales give young readers the stories of Shakespeare's plays. Fourteen – all of the comedies – are by Mary Lamb, while Charles, better known now as an essayist, wrote the tragedies. They were published by M. J. Godwin and Co., the children's book publishing business that William Godwin and his second wife, Mary Jane, founded. Only Charles's name is on the title page. There were two reasons for the omission of hers: Charles, unlike his sister, had an established literary reputation and his name would sell books; and Mary, who suffered from intermittent psychosis, had stabbed her mother to death in a fit of madness in 1796.

This was the deciding event of both Charles's and Mary Lamb's lives, and the brother protected and cared for his older sister until his death almost forty years later. She, in return, cared for him and did the work that a wife and housekeeper might otherwise have done. Mary Lamb was perfectly lucid between bouts of madness, which became regular, recurring about once a year, often in reaction to especially difficult situations. The necessary quietness of her life

Grave tales

Mary Lamb wrote little during a life blighted by mental illness. The frontispiece of Mrs. Leicester's School *(London, 1809) shows an orphan girl learning to read from her mother's gravestone. This macabre image is thought to have inspired the equally macabre opening of Charles Dickens's* Great Expectations *(1861).*

PFORZHEIMER COLLECTION

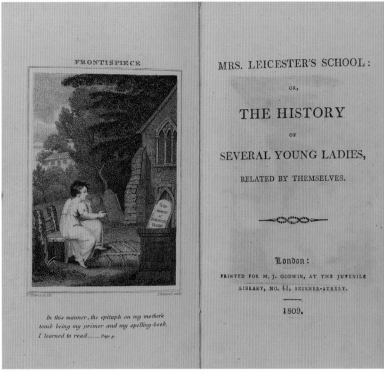

FRONTISPIECE

MRS. LEICESTER'S SCHOOL:

OR,

THE HISTORY

OF

SEVERAL YOUNG LADIES,

RELATED BY THEMSELVES.

London:

PRINTED FOR M. J. GODWIN, AT THE JUVENILE LIBRARY, NO. 41, SKINNER-STREET.

1809.

In this manner, the epitaph on my mother's tomb being my primer and my spelling-book, I learned to read.___Page 9.

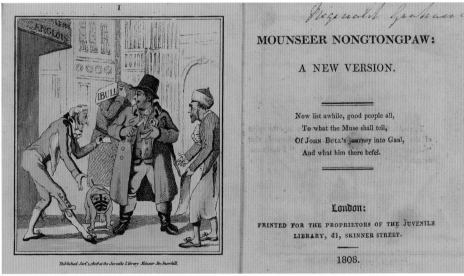

MOUNSEER NONGTONGPAW:

A NEW VERSION.

Now list awhile, good people all,
To what the Muse shall tell,
Of JOHN BULL's journey into Gaul,
And what him there befel.

London:

PRINTED FOR THE PROPRIETORS OF THE JUVENILE LIBRARY, 41, SKINNER STREET.

1808.

A chapbook for children

The future Mary Shelley had only a small part in writing Mounseer Nongtongpaw: or The Discoveries of John Bull in a Trip to Paris *(London, 1808), but it was the beginning of a lifelong career. This chapbook for children was a humorous take-off on British tourists in Paris. The unsophisticated John Bull thinks that "Monsieur, je ne vous entends pas" ("Sir, I don't understand you") is the name of a very great person, since it is the reply to every question he asks.* PFORZHEIMER COLLECTION

meant that she was not as productive as she might have been. She had no encouragement from Charles, who disliked even the idea of lady writers working independently of their brothers. This is a shame, since her writing (like Charles Lamb's) has considerable charm. *Mrs. Leicester's School*, her other major work, came out soon after the *Tales from Shakespear*, and features young girls telling the stories of their lives. The frontispiece, depicting a young boy on the grave of his father, is said to have inspired the opening of Charles Dickens's *Great Expectations* (1861), in which the hero Pip visits his parents' graves.[18]

Mary Lamb was at least able to develop these works fully. She is also the author of a brief essay, "On Needle-Work," in which a number of pregnant observations are made: she notices, for example, that women's continual employment at needlework means that they are never hard at work but never quite at leisure either. And while their time is eaten up by sewing for the family, they usurp what might have been a lucrative occupation for poor women. These were progressive thoughts, and it is our loss that they are confined to a brief essay by a woman whose claim to being extraordinary has such unfortunate origins.

VISUAL ARTISTS

While women took the front of the field in prose fiction, they made smaller advances as artists. Painting and sculpting are difficult to do unobtrusively or privately, and to do them with any seriousness requires considerable outlays of money for supplies. However, a number of women were successful professional artists in Britain during these years, and a much larger number were enthusiastic amateurs.

The amateurs grew in number because art education was extremely popular in these years. British travelers and collectors, such as Sir William Hamilton, among many others, had for decades been bringing back art from their Grand Tours of Europe, whether it was bought, commissioned, bartered, or (as happened during the Napoleonic Wars) pillaged. Although their sisters rarely went along, the women appreciated their brothers' acquisitions when the shipping crates were opened. Closer to home, the picturesque movement allowed women, and anyone with an eye, to find picturesque landscapes in their back gardens – or, at least, within Britain. This was done by applying the laws of painting to the natural prospect that lay before the viewer: Catherine Morland, heroine of Austen's *Northanger Abbey*, learns how to look for "foregrounds, distances, and second distances – side-screens and perspectives – lights and shades" as she climbs Beechen Cliff, and by the time she reaches the top "voluntarily reject[s] the whole city of Bath, as unworthy to make part of the landscape."[19] Austen is joking, of course; but the picturesque movement and the neoclassical strain in art made it common and fashionable for young girls to know how to sketch and paint as well as how to look at pictures.

Angelica Kauffmann (1741–1807)

The rise of the educated amateur may also have made it easier for the relatively few women who practiced art professionally in Britain. The Swiss-born Angelica Kauffmann arrived in Britain with all possible advantages: she was beautiful, well-connected, and had the best artistic education Italy could give – except for painting the human figure from nature (that is, in the nude). She quickly became the most famous woman artist of her time, and – partly thanks to her friendship with Sir Joshua Reynolds – was a founding member of the Royal Academy of the Arts in 1768. However, when Johann Zoffany executed a group portrait of those members in 1771–72, he represented Kauffmann and the single other female academician, the flower painter Mary Moser, only as portraits on the wall – pictures within the picture. This was because the male academicians were portrayed in the midst of arranging how a naked male model should sit while they sketched him. There may be more than a hint of irony in a mural that Kauffmann painted years later for the ceiling of the Royal Academy's central hall, in which the allegorical figure of Design is shown learning how to draw, not from a live model, but from the fragmentary torso of a male statue.[20]

Kauffmann's success was considerable, as were her artistic gifts. Born in Switzerland to an artist father who encouraged her from earliest childhood, she was a prodigy, and executed her first commissioned portraits at the age of eleven. Johann Josef Kauffmann took the girl to Italy, the world center for the visual arts; there, during her education and early career, Kauffmann continued to paint portraits, and within a year after she moved to London, her commissions had brought in enough income to enable her to buy a house. She made a first marriage, later annulled, to a German impostor pretending to be a count. Beyond this unsettling episode, Kauffmann managed her career adroitly, and painted her share of the grand-scale historical works that British and French artists made to show that they had arrived.

At the same time, she used her femininity to make opportunities that would not have been so easily available to men. *Angelica's Ladies Library* was her own version of the gift annual, that most feminine of all genres. The annuals were a steady source of hackwork for professional writers; Mary Shelley and Letitia Landon both wrote for them to support their children.

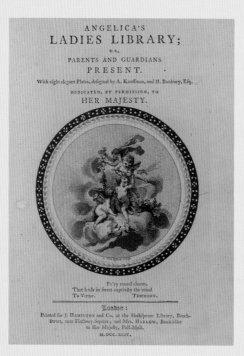

A Swiss painter in London

Angelica Kauffmann had early success in both London and Italy. She was one of only two women elected to London's Royal Academy of the Arts on its founding in 1768. In addition to her oil paintings and engravings, she also published a gift book: Angelica's Ladies Library (London, 1794) was a handsome instrument by which to keep her name and work before the public eye. PFORZHEIMER COLLECTION; Angelica Kauffmann Pittrice, *engraving by A. Testa, after Angelica Kauffmann, undated.*
PRINT COLLECTION

Kauffmann, who had a happy second marriage with an Italian painter, was childless and did not need to turn to the annuals for cash. Her energetic professional life, continuing after her return to Italy, shows rather that she was passionate about her work, and at her funeral, two of her paintings were carried to show, better than any coffin might, what had been lost.

Lady Diana Beauclerk (1734–1808)

If her income had equalled her rank, Lady Diana Beauclerk, daughter of the Duke of Marlborough, would not have had to provide for herself.[21] She was born Lady Diana Spencer and known universally as Lady Di, like her descendant and namesake, the late ex-wife of Prince Charles. Her first marriage to Frederick St. John Bolingbroke, Viscount Bolingbroke,[22] was unhappy and plagued by his drinking, philandering, and gambling debts. They had already obtained a legal separation when she became pregnant by Topham Beauclerk, a book collector and friend of Samuel Johnson's; a divorce from Bolingbroke by act of Parliament followed in 1768, and Diana married Beauclerk two days later. The second marriage proved as unhappy as the first, although Lady Di nursed Beauclerk at the pathetic end of his life, when he was crawling with lice and addicted to laudanum. He died in 1780 after years of bad health. There were children by both men, and money difficulties. Diana, at forty-six a middle-aged single mother, turned to her artistic skills to help pay the bills.

Lady Diana's artistic labors had begun even before Topham Beauclerk's death threw her on her own resources, and her family connections proved extremely useful at the beginning of what became a genuinely professional career. But she did not become a professional in the same way that Angelica Kauffmann did; for one thing, Diana Beauclerk did not work much in oils, preferring pastels and watercolors, genteel media in which girls of her station would have been taught as a matter of course. Second, she made canny use of her connections in aristocratic circles. A charming watercolor portrait of her second cousin, Georgiana, the Duchess of Devonshire, was engraved by Francesco Bartolozzi, the most celebrated engraver of his day. It was then published, not merely printed for friends and family. Two hundred copies were made, a large edition for the time; they were "snapped up by society and rapidly sold out."[23] This occurred while the scandal of Diana's divorce and swift remarriage was still hot, and it was kind of Georgiana to allow her portrait to be thus circulated. The scheme itself originated apparently not with Lady Diana but with her brother, the Duke of Marlborough, and only Bartolozzi profited from the venture. However, its success was balm to Lady Diana's sexual reputation and a boost to her artistic one. This was only the first of many pictures that she had engraved, and in time Lady Di reversed the financial relationship: while amateurs might pay to have their works engraved, the normal procedure for professionals was to sell the rights to the engraver or etcher, who then made his (or her, for there were a few professional female engravers) profit from the copies.[24]

The Duchess of Devonshire was not Lady Diana's only advocate; for years, her friend Horace Walpole, the collector, championed her work enthusiastically, even to the point of eccentricity. For his pleasure, Lady Diana illustrated in 1775–76 his play *The Mysterious Mother*. Walpole was so taken with her ink-and-wash drawings that he added a tiny room devoted to them – the "Beauclerk Closet" – to his Gothic mansion at Strawberry Hill, and took only the most privileged guests to see them. Later, for pay, Lady Di would illustrate Edmund Spenser's Arthurian epic, *The Faerie Queene*; John Dryden's *Fables Ancient and Modern*; and the German poet Gottfried Bürgher's ballad *Leonora*, in which a young woman elopes with a man she believes to be her fiancé but who is, in fact, Death.

Impoverished aristocrat

If her income had equalled her rank, Lady Diana Beauclerk would not have had to provide for herself. As it was, she fell into considerable debt. Her relative, Georgiana, Duchess of Devonshire, helped Diana to establish her name as an artist by allowing her to market prints of a portrait Diana had made of her. Georgiana, Duchess of Devonshire, *mezzotint by Robert Laurie, after Lady Diana Beauclerk, 1779.* PRINT COLLECTION

Finally, one more source of Lady Diana Beauclerk's income merits mention here, since it drew her into the rapidly expanding world of consumer goods in late eighteenth-century Britain. Josiah Wedgwood, industrialist, inventor, and entrepreneur, produced lines of china at his pottery in Staffordshire using Greek and Roman motifs for which he drew ideas from, among others, the collection of Sir William Hamilton. Ann Radcliffe's father sold his wares in Bath. Wedgwood also employed aristocratic women as designers, since "their work would be ... in tune with the customers' needs, [and] there could be useful publicity in using such women."[25] Lady Diana was ideally suited for this work: small-scale scenes of gods, goats, and garlands were one of her specialties, and her name was certainly well known. Her designs were popular and sold briskly, as Wedgwood china still does.

LEONORA.

TRANSLATED FROM

THE GERMAN

OF

GOTTFRIED AUGUSTUS BÜRGHER,

BY

W. R. SPENCER, Esq.

WITH

DESIGNS

BY

THE RIGHT HONOURABLE

LADY DIANA BEAUCLERC.

LONDON:
PRINTED BY T. BENSLEY;
FOR J. EDWARDS, AND E. AND S. HARDING, PALL MALL.

1796.

Romantic illustrator

In later years, Lady Di was a well-known illustrator. Gottfried Bürgher's Leonora, *a tale of a maiden carried off by Death, was popular with Romantic audiences, and Lady Diana's 1796 edition, its frontispiece mixing putti and skeletons, was quite successful.*

PFORZHEIMER COLLECTION

None of Lady Diana's labor saved her from a relatively impoverished old age, although she did not go hungry or die in debt. Her last years were made both harder and easier by the responsibility for a granddaughter, whom she loved dearly and who, she saw to it, learned how to draw.

Anne Seymour Damer (1749–1828)

Horace Walpole's other favorite female artist was his cousin Anne Damer, an amateur sculptor; he wrote of both Damer and Beauclerk to a mutual friend, the travel writer Mary Berry, "I defy your favourite Italy to produce ... such monuments of female genius."[26] Sculpting was a more unusual avocation than painting, although the actress Sarah Siddons followed it as well; but Anne Damer was an unusual woman. While still a child, she was challenged by the philosopher David Hume, a family friend, to do better than a sculptor whose work Anne scorned when they saw it on the street. She rose to the challenge immediately, and the evidence of her talent induced her parents to have her taught by the major sculptors of the day. By no means was everyone in agreement with Walpole's assessment of her gifts. Maria Callcott, a travel writer and historian (discussed further in Chapter Seven), reported that as a little girl visiting Strawberry Hill, she would watch with great interest "the progress of that very good-natured woman, but very bad sculptor, in spoiling marble."[27] This is too harsh, as Walpole is too enthusiastic: the sculptures that survive are the work of a competent amateur who manages to catch a likeness of her sitter without succeeding in making the work speak beyond its own limits.

Like Diana Beauclerk, she married unhappily; Anne Damer's marriage ended even worse than Diana's two, when her husband, deeply in debt, shot himself. She did not remarry. Rumors persistently linked her with Elizabeth Farren, an actress who eventually married the Earl of Derby, to the extent that Derby asked his betrothed to stop seeing Mrs. Damer.[28] It is true that Anne Damer made a bust of Elizabeth Farren, but she made many busts – of the scientist Sir Joseph Banks, for instance, as well as Charles James Fox and Emma Hamilton's lover, Horatio, Lord Nelson. It's also true, however, that Damer sounds like a modern lesbian of a certain type. Joseph Farington, an artist and diarist, describes her as "singular": "She wears a Mans Hat, and Shoes, – and a Jacket also like a mans – thus she walks ab[out]t. the fields with a hooking stick."[29] Maria Callcott writes that "it is well known that her appearance and voice were anything but feminine."[30] While Damer apparently had a romantic friendship with Mary Berry, she might also be said to have had a romantic friendship with Horace Walpole: while their relationship was certainly not sexual, it was filled with mutual admiration, and she lived nearby him for many years. Walpole, in his will, left his beloved Strawberry Hill to Damer for her lifetime along with money for its maintenance.

Besides her friends, the main passion of Anne Damer's life seem to have been dogs – which she sculpted – and, of course, sculpture itself. And however singular she was, she was perfectly schooled in the manners of her class. A few minutes after she had been slightly injured in a fall from a scaffold surrounding her work in progress, an eight-foot-high image of George III, her mother and a friend came to visit the studio. She braved out their visit amidst their admiring, if slightly obtuse, remarks of "Lord! What a charming scaffold! What a delightful scaffold! So clever; was there ever anything so clever, so well contrived?" and hid her pain until she found herself fainting.[31] She was buried, at her own direction, with her sculptor's apron, tools, and the ashes of her favorite dog in her coffin.

Chapter Six

RATIONAL DAMES AND LADIES ON HORSEBACK: SCIENTISTS AND TRAVELERS

THE ROMANTIC ERA afforded rich opportunities to young women with a passion for science or mathematics. The years between 1789 and 1837 were crucial in the history of science and technology, and both men and women, girls and boys, studied these fields with great interest (in the same way that computers have been a matter of interest to more or less everyone since, say, 1975: people in the midst of a revolution are well aware that it is taking place). The novelist Maria Edgeworth, writing in 1795, observed: "Instead of being ashamed that so little has been hitherto done by female abilities, in science and useful literature, I am surprised that so much has been effected."[1] The women presented here who devoted themselves to studying the natural world are among the most outward-looking of this book. The chapter concludes with a trio who not only looked out beyond their own lives but traveled far from their homes and, in one way or another, transmitted their experiences to later readers.

SCIENTISTS

Science education was not yet an important part of the curriculum at the (still all-male) universities. In England, Oxford and Cambridge were just branching out from an exclusive emphasis on the classics, and even medical education was second-rate. (At the Scottish universities, however, medicine was a traditional strength.) But neither science nor technology was part of a gentleman's formal education in Britain. One result of this was that careers in science and technology were open to intelligent and driven working- and middle-class boys like Josiah Wedgwood or his fellow industrialist Matthew Boulton, while careers in, say, diplomacy or politics were not. Serious work in science was rarely possible for working-class girls, whose opportunities were circumscribed by both gender and class. But there are exceptions even here: Mary Anning (1799–1847), a pioneer paleontologist, began at age twelve to dig for fossils in the sea cliffs near her native Lyme Regis, to provide for her family after her father's death. Among other discoveries, she unearthed over time a pleiosaurus, an ichthyosaurus, and a pterodactyl. She was eventually made an honorary fellow of the Royal Geological Society.

Another result of the sciences' freedom from the academic cage was that their pursuit was viewed as an improving and innocent pastime for genteel young women. There were a number of conduits of knowledge. Girls could read from a wide range of books written specifically for them; favorite subjects in the mid-eighteenth century included geology, chemistry, entomology, and conchology, which was abetted by the fashion, among those with estates, for "gothic" grottoes walled or decorated with shells.[2] Toward the end of the century, botany was made popular by Priscilla Wakefield's 1796 *Introduction to Botany*. Volumes on zoology,

Higher education

The teacher and author Margaret Bryan ran a series of successful schools for girls, teaching the sciences at such a high level that her students sometimes needed coaching sessions to understand her lectures. She is portrayed here with her daughters in the frontispiece of her Compendious System of Astronomy *(London, 1797). The plate, from her* Lectures on Natural Philosophy *(London, 1806), illustrates a lesson in optics.* PFORZHEIMER COLLECTION

mineralogy, and ornithology also appeared, sometimes aimed at very small children, such as *The Rational Dame; or, Hints Towards Supplying Prattle for Children*, by Ellenor Fenn ("Mrs. Lovechild"), which gave lessons in natural history for toddlers.

Older girls might continue learning sciences that demanded greater application and more mathematical expertise, such as chemistry and astronomy. Undertaking scientific work seriously required money and was made considerably easier by support from others; most of the few women who became professional or quasi-professional scientists had had, as women artists did, the steady sponsorship of one key family member, most often a man. But many of the more serious girls' schools also taught science, and some, such as Margaret Bryan's, specialized in it. Bryan, who ran girls' schools in London and later in the seaside town of Margate, published not only a *Compendious System of Astronomy* but, nine years later, an equally large volume of *Lectures on Natural Philosophy* – two books in very different realms of knowledge. The "natural philosophy" of the second title was the common term for what is now generally called science, and the lectures emphasize physics, mechanics, and optics. Both volumes were based on Bryan's class notes; coaching, she wrote, was sometimes necessary to allow her students to understand the more abstruse lectures. Judging from the impressive subscription lists for both books, and the fact that the second is dedicated by permission to Charlotte, Princess of Wales, Bryan's school must have done very well. (Charlotte, one hopes, enjoyed Bryan's book more than she did Hannah More's, though in its way it is no less demanding.)

Beyond these venues for learning, young girls would also have found scientific articles and mathematical problems for readers posed in the pages of ladies' magazines. Outings to workshops, laboratories, factories, and mines were a common practice – indeed, it "seems to have been taken for granted that women would like to know the intimate details of industrial processes."[5] One of the most celebrated of these destinations in the late 1780s was William Herschel's forty-foot telescope at Slough, near Windsor and thus convenient for visits from the king and queen, who were keenly interested in its progress. The tube of the instrument, then the largest telescope in the world, was in fact thirty-nine feet four inches; before its mirrors and lenses were installed in 1789, it was extremely fashionable to take a stroll through it. Frances Burney did so in July 1786, and reported that she could have gone through upright "dressed in feather and bell-hoop."[4] After its completion, William Herschel would report his findings in the night sky by means of a speaking tube to his sister Caroline, who waited for them in a little hut at the bottom.

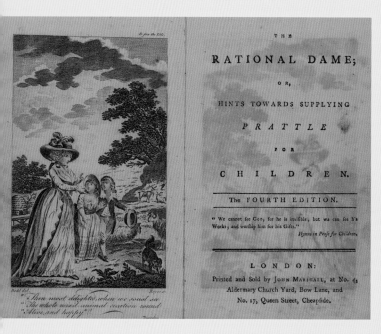

Zoology for toddlers

The vogue for teaching science at home extended even to works for very small children, and with The Rational Dame; or, Hints Towards Supplying Prattle for Children *(London, 1790), Ellenor Fenn (1743–1813) – a.k.a. Mrs. Lovechild – produced a volume of elementary zoology for the under-six set. Many of the images appealed to children's love for small furry creatures.*
PFORZHEIMER COLLECTION

Science at home

An Introduction to Botany *(London, 1798), by the conservative writer Priscilla Wakefield (1751–1832), helped to start a fashion for scientific learning among genteel girls and women. Since science was only beginning to be taught at universities, there was no social reason for girls not to study it, and fields like botany, entomology, mineralogy, and paleology, among others, could easily be pursued from home.* PFORZHEIMER COLLECTION

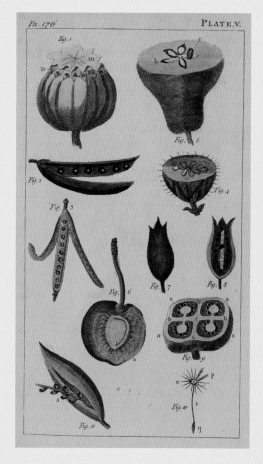

Caroline Herschel
(1750–1848)

There is little doubt that if William (1738–1822) had not needed, as he did, considerable assistance in his nightly sweeping of the skies, Caroline would not have become an astronomer. William Herschel remains one of the most important of all astronomers, known for extending the science beyond the solar system and into the stars. Indeed, at the beginning of his career the solar system numbered one planet fewer than it does now, for Herschel, in addition to discovering over two thousand nebulae, was the first human being to see the planet Uranus. In an attempt to fortify his friendly relations with the king (a fellow-Hanoverian, after all, and his major source of funding), he called it the Georgium Sidus, the star of George.

Caroline Herschel nearly became one of the millions of women who have spent their lives in traceless housework. The Herschels, a German family of musicians from Hanover, had ten children. Caroline, the eighth, was a tiny creature who stood only four feet three inches as an adult. Her mother singled her out of the brood to act as servant to the older children and to take care of the general household cleaning. Although her father gave her some violin lessons on the sly, her mother wished her to have as little education as possible to prevent her from getting above her station, and strenuously obstructed Caroline's attempts to learn even enough to become a governess.

William had moved to England, becoming the organist of the fashionable Octagon Chapel in Bath in 1766, an employment that also entailed directing concerts

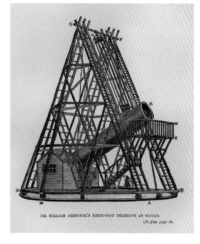

SIR WILLIAM HERSCHEL'S FORTY-FOOT TELESCOPE AT SLOUGH.
[*To face page 39.*]

Sweeping the skies
Caroline Herschel looked patiently, night after night, for comets, discovering eight new ones over the years. She performed celestial housework out of devotion to her brother William, still one of the giants of astronomy, who (among other accomplishments) revolutionized the design of telescopes. His forty-foot telescope, shown here in an illustration from the Memoir and Correspondence of Caroline Herschel *(London, 1876), attracted keen interest from tourists in the 1780s, including the king and queen.* GENERAL RESEARCH DIVISION

and oratorios. In 1772 he brought Caroline over from Hanover, her fine soprano voice half-trained by her own efforts. She received further training in England and began what might have been a rather successful singing career. It was at just this time, however, that Herschel's supernal intelligence led him to give up music in favor of astronomy and the making of telescopes; by 1782 he was devoting his whole time to two ambitions: "to carry improvements in telescopes to their utmost extent" and "to leave no spot of the heavens unexamined."[5]

And not just his own time: although she was understandably vexed at first on finding her singing career suddenly ended in favor of long hours aiding in the production and employment of telescopes, Caroline too was drawn into the effort through her devotion to the brother who had rescued her from life as a menial servant. As one biography notes, "he took her away from a life of monotonous drudgery and gave her a life of interesting drudgery."[6] If her mother had not made her into a housewife, she had given her daughter a degree of self-abnegation extraordinary even when this quality was valued in women as it is not now; she claimed that she "had done nothing for him [William] but what a well-trained puppy-dog would have done."[7] There was no occupation that she considered demeaning: when William had to sit for hours at a stretch polishing the huge round mirrors, seven feet or more across, by which the telescopes functioned, she fed him by hand and read aloud from novels. To construct the mold for the tube of the forty-foot telescope, hundreds of pounds of dried horse manure had to be sifted, and Caroline Herschel was one of the crew who sifted – twice, since the first mold cracked on being filled with molten metal. She also made the notations of each night's discovery and did the considerable mathematical work necessary to record the locations of stars.

Eventually, Caroline Herschel was given a smaller telescope of her own and asked to sweep the heavens, looking for comets on nights when William did not need her. (The irony of the housewifely term need not be avoided, but to "sweep" in this sense means to search systematically across a carefully noted area of the night sky.) This coincided with her being displaced as William's housekeeper by the event of his marriage in 1788; she had never lived without him since arriving in England. The brother and sister were far from wholly severed, however; Caroline Herschel lived near William and his wife. Left alone, her astronomical work became paramount, and it was during her solitary watches that she discovered the comets – eight altogether – for which she is still remembered. Her achievements as an astronomer also included assisting William in the discovery of a thousand double stars, and the cataloguing of many more.

Despite her bent for self-denial, Caroline Herschel was publicly appreciated in her lifetime; when, in 1787, William was awarded a grant of £2,000 toward the completion of his forty-foot telescope, and £200 for its up-keep, another £50 per annum was included as a salary for his assistant. The initial installment was, she wrote, "the first money I ever in all my lifetime thought myself to be at liberty to spend to my own liking."[8] Unfortunately, it was the only installment paid.[9] In 1828, after his death, she was awarded the gold medal of the Royal Astronomical Society, in honor of her catalogue of the star clusters and nebulae that she and William had observed, and in 1835 the Society made her an honorary fellow – the best sort of fellowship to which a woman could then aspire.

By that time she had returned to Hanover, where she went soon after William's death in 1822, giving up most of her small income to another brother before she left. Caroline Herschel ceased sweeping the skies on her return to Germany, although this may have caused her regret; her cataloguing work continued into her seventies. She remained vividly interested in astronomy to the end of her life, and the strong bonds between her and her nephew, the astronomer Sir John Herschel, were intellectual as well as emotional. In her nineties, she would amuse herself by picturing "a whole solar system in one corner of her room," giving "to each newly-discovered star its proper place."[10] She was awarded the gold medal for science by the king of Prussia in 1846 and died in full possession of her faculties at ninety-seven.

Anna Atkins (1799–1871)

Anna Atkins's *Photographs of British Algae: Cyanotype Impressions* (1843–53) represents a peak achievement in the accomplishments of amateur women scientists of the Romantic period. Her great work, illustrating hundreds of different species of seaweed, is so beautiful that its images hover on the boundary between science and art. It is also exceedingly rare, both as to its mode, the cyanotype photogram, and in itself, since she made probably fewer than twenty copies.[11]

Atkins was also unusual in that she was working alone. She had, however, encouragement and company from infancy, since Anna Children was born in Kent to a scientific family. Her mother, Hester Anne Holwell, died before her daughter was a year old. Her father, John George Children, was a zoologist and curator of, successively, the natural history and zoological collections of the British Museum; he was also a Fellow of the Royal Society, the first and most general of the royal scientific societies. Children was kind and sociable, and through him and through a childhood friend, Anna Hatchett, whose father was a chemist, Anna Children grew up surrounded by scientists and scientific work. She also received training in art and, in her early twenties, illustrated her father's translation of Lamarck's *Genera of Shells*, working at a professional level of accuracy and detail on images of 250 different species. In 1825 she became Anna Atkins, marrying a friend of her father's who shared and supported her interests.

Atkins learned about photography directly from William Henry Fox Talbot, its British pioneer and a family friend. The announcement of its invention in 1839 was greeted with great interest and enthusiasm in Britain and all of Europe; inventors had been trying for years to perfect a photographic process. The technical difficulty was not the taking of photographs but finding a means by which to make them permanent. This was solved by William Herschel's only child, John, now Sir John Herschel, who had devised a photographic fixer.

A brilliant astronomer himself and another friend of the Atkins and Children families, Herschel was also the inventor of the cyanotype process, which he communicated to John Children soon after its coming into being. Cyanotypes are properly termed photograms rather than photographs, since the objects to be recorded – seaweed, in this case – were laid directly onto chemically treated paper. (Photographic negatives could also be printed by being laid on the paper.) The image was then exposed for fifteen minutes or so to the sun, and "fixed," made permanent, with ordinary water, which brought out the deep blue color. This simplicity gave the process great flexibility: no darkroom was required, the paper was simply brushed with the requisite chemicals, and the results were stable, not prone to deteriorate as photographs sometimes did. Its drawback is that images are always, and only, light blue on an aquamarine background, in itself a delicious combination, but not flattering to images of the human face: "a portrait reproduced in shades of blue took on ghastly qualities."[12] It is now used commonly only for architectural blueprints.

The process was, however, perfect for a botanist who wanted to make an extensive visual record of the seaweeds that appeared on the shores of Britain. It was more precise and less time-consuming than drawing, and it was manageable by a single person. Atkins embarked on *British Algae* in 1843, a year after Herschel had first sent news of the cyanotype process. The work appeared in parts over a ten-year period, with Atkins suspending production for a year after her much-loved father died, in order to write a biography of him. While it has been called the first British book illustrated with photographs – and certainly it is a contender for that title – *British Algae* was not really published.[13] Atkins, a true amateur, made up copies for individual friends or institutions, and distributed them free of charge.

It is clear that "the collecting, preparing, and subsequent handling of the specimens probably constituted the most difficult part of the production of *British Algae*."[14] We have no photograph of Atkins at work, and can only imagine her watchfully roving the shore at low tide, shod in newly invented Wellington boots, the hem of her long dress dragging in the brine, basket under her arm, cleaning specimens while they were still in the water, as algae collectors agreed was the easiest method.[15] They were then dried in a press between thick sheets of paper, as flowers are, and identified from the standard work on the subject, William Harvey's *Manual of British Algae* (1841). The process of exposing the specimens and paper to the sun, then washing the paper and setting it to dry flat, would have been relatively easy.

Like Caroline Herschel's sweeping of the stars, this was repetitive, painstaking, time-engrossing work. Also like the star-sweeping, however, it gave the seeker a constant, purposeful exposure to objects of beauty and interest, and the possibility of finding something entirely new. Atkins's work, though, was all

Blue beauty

Anna Atkins, an amateur marine botanist, took care of every aspect of her masterpiece,
Photographs of British Algae: Cyanotype Impressions *(1843–53): she collected hundreds
of specimens of seaweed, and identified, labelled, and photographed them, employing
the cyanotype process (now used only for blueprints). Then, working from her home
in Sevenoaks, Kent, she arranged them into a series of volumes. Shown here are a title
page and three species of seaweed:* Laminaria digitata, Gelideum corneum, *and*
Sargassum plumosum. SPENCER COLLECTION

her own. She worked under no one's direction and for no one else's glory. When the *Algae* was complete, she did not retire or cease photographing, but moved on to other projects "of a much wider variety of subjects, demonstrating a heightened visual awareness."[16] Women scientists with leisure, self-direction, and self-possession might thus find that the end of one task could mean moving forward and seeing more.

Augusta Ada Byron King, Countess of Lovelace (1815–1852)

Ada Byron might have inherited from her father, the poet George Gordon Byron, Lord Byron, the self-possession needed for a mathematical career: some of her letters show her full of confidence in her mind's power, and she took to mathematics with enthusiasm. However, her mother, the former Anna Isabella Milbanke (known as Annabella), had such fondness for minute control of everyone in her household, from the kitchen maids to her daughter, that if self-possession were to be possible at all for Ada, it would have to be obtained by theft. Her place in mathematical history derives largely from what she perceived, rather than what she did, but in her case being far-sighted was sufficient. Augusta Ada Byron King, Countess of Lovelace, saw that her friend Charles Babbage's Difference Engine and Analytical Engine might change dramatically how scientific work was conducted: "in so distributing and combining the truths and the formulae of analysis ... the relations and the nature of many subjects ... are necessarily thrown into new lights, and more profoundly investigated."[17] In other words, Ada Byron saw, well before electric lighting had been invented, the implications of the computer.

Her childhood both prepared her for such a vision and left her unable to make as much of it as she might have. Ada's parents, George Gordon Byron, Lord Byron (1788–1824) and Lady Annabella (1792–1860), were separated just after her birth, and the child never knew her father. Lady Byron's style of mother-love may be illustrated by her slicing open the infant Ada's gums to let the teeth grow in more easily. She was a steadfast believer in frequent bleeding and leeching, and, as she grew older, in a variety of Christianity that emphasized sin and guilt. Her daughter's biographer describes her as the "very personification" of "discord and implacability," and she seems to have combined unconscious sadism with the impulse to control the lives of all around her.[18] While Ada had some tremendous advantages in her birth and station, she was unlucky indeed in her mother.

Perhaps the single non-material advantage that Lady Byron transmitted to her daughter was a talent for mathematics, and the girl's gift in the subject was encouraged (and managed) from the start. And while her girlhood was far from happy, Ada had moments of pleasure. She was often taken on tours of sites of industrial and technical innovations, and while she had few companions of her own age, she kept company with the daughters of William Frend, who had tutored Lady Byron in astronomy, geometry, and algebra. She loved riding, and at nineteen wrote to Mary Somerville that "being on a leaping horse was the greatest pleasure she knew, 'even better than waltzing.'"[19]

Her acquaintance with Mary Somerville (1780–1872) was one of her great pleasures, for Somerville was the most celebrated woman scientist of her time. A polymath, she wrote on astronomy, mathematics, physics, chemistry, mineralogy, and geology, among other subjects, on a level suitable for professionals as well as amateurs. Her most successful book, *On the Connexion of the Physical Sciences* (1834), brought all these subjects together; Somerville continued to revise and expand it throughout her lifetime, incorporating changes in the disciplines as they developed. She met Ada when the girl was in her teens, and encouraged her to study mathematics; Ada responded warmly and sent her questions to Somerville when she met with any difficulty.[20] It was, indeed, through Mary Somerville's son that Ada met her future husband, William King, Lord King, later the Earl of Lovelace.

If Ada Byron had been born in 1830 instead of 1815, she might have gone to Queen's College, the first English college for women, in 1848, its opening year. As it was, King genuinely appreciated his wife's mind, and was not the worst choice Ada could have made, although he showed himself unhappily susceptible to Lady Byron's

A head for numbers
Ada Byron's gift for numbers revealed itself early. She inherited poetic imagination from her father, Lord Byron, but employed it in mathematical pursuits. As the married Countess of Lovelace, she supported the inventor Charles Babbage, whose Difference Engine and Analytical Engine were fore-runners of the computer. The Countess herself developed an early version of a programming language; the United States Department of Defense named a language ADA in her honor. This anonymous watercolor from about 1835 shows her soon after she met Babbage. PFORZHEIMER COLLECTION

influence. Later in their marriage, he had himself elected to the Royal Society to gain at least indirect access for Ada to its books and papers. Mary Somerville's husband, William, performed research and bibliographical duties at the Royal Society's library for his wife as well; and more than one writer has noted the irony that both men, in doing so, would have passed the bust of Mary Somerville that stood in her honor in the Society's entrance hall. The barring of women from scientific societies was a point of sore contention throughout the second half of the nineteenth century, and both Byron and Somerville were on the edge of the change.

The most significant person in Ada Byron's scientific acquaintance, the mathematician Charles Babbage (1791–1871), supported the entry of women into the new British Association for the Advancement of Science, founded in 1831. He did not carry his point then – and he made it out of the wish to be chivalrous, not egalitarian – but women did eventually join simply by dint of continuing to show up in large numbers at its conferences.[21] Babbage had given up a professorship at Cambridge to devote himself full time to his calculating machines. (John Herschel was a friend from university days and encouraged him in their early development.) Babbage had built one such machine, the Difference Engine, and had received considerable funding from the British government to work on it. At the time he met Ada, during her brief London season before marriage, he had turned to a more ambitious and sophisticated project, the Analytical Engine. Unlike the Difference Engine, which "was a mechanical device for computing and printing tables of mathematical functions by addition," the Analytical Engine could "add, subtract, multiply, and divide directly, and the plans called for programming it with punched cards."[22] Ada had listened with great interest to lectures on Babbage's "engines" before she met him, and courted his acquaintance for their sake as well as his own – for Babbage was "very good company, and much sought after in the best society."[23] She sought to make him her tutor in mathematics, and failing in this – his working life was single-mindedly devoted to his machines – taught herself the branches of mathematics needed to understand their workings. Meanwhile, she and Babbage became friends; he had considerable support from those who did not understand what he was doing, but was grateful to be supported by someone who did.

Ada's – now the Countess of Lovelace's – greatest contribution to the enterprise came when she translated from the French, in late 1842, a detailed description of the Analytical Engine, its principles and mechanisms. With Babbage's encouragement she added seven "notes" of her own, not mere footnotes but additional short papers concerning her original work on programming the machine; she had also written several programs "for performing advanced mathematical calculations."[24] (Because of her particular concern with this aspect of computing, the United States Department of Defense named one of its programming languages ADA.) The work was published under her initials in *Taylor's Scientific Memoirs* for 1843.

Mary Somerville had, as she saw herself, "perseverance and intelligence, but no genius," and attributed this lack to her sex, which she saw as "of the earth, earthy."[25] Ada saw no such flaw in herself; she wrote to Babbage that she was "quite thunderstruck" at the power of her own prose in the paper for *Taylor's*; she saw it as "unlike a *woman's* style surely but neither can I compare it with any man's exactly."[26] She might later have done work to justify her own hubris. As it is, she fell soon after the publication of the notes into a dependence on opium, morphine, and alcohol, none of which was considered terribly dangerous at the time; they were simply painkillers, routinely prescribed or purchased over the counter. Ada's strength of mind is shown by the fact that she overcame this dependence on her own.[27]

It was replaced by an addiction to gambling on horses; Babbage, among others, helped her to place her bets, as she could not have done so on her own. The days when the Duchess of Devonshire pursued gaming at the private homes of her friends had passed; but the need to conceal one's losses from one's husband had not, and the Countess of Lovelace had also a monstrous mother to contend with. The drawn-out disaster of her gambling was interrupted by a still worse one, her early death from cancer, made all the more torturous by Lady Byron's refusal to let her have morphine or opium, since Ada's pain was manifestly a sign of sin. Her death, like her father's, came too young; but while he had an extraordinarily productive life, his daughter's was doubly tragic because she was so largely prevented from carrying out what she might have done.

TRAVELERS

Unlike science, travel for women alone was expensive, difficult, and relatively rare in the Romantic period. For everyone, the French Revolution and the Napoleonic Wars made journeys to France and much of the rest of continental Europe difficult between 1793 and 1815. Young men who could not make the traditional Grand Tour found alternatives; but young women had never made the Grand Tour. The women presented below, then, can be seen as genuine pioneers in a way that the scientists described above are not, although both groups were following a similar impetus to grasp more of the world through their own experience.

While women in the sciences grew rarer as the nineteenth century continued, and today are severely underrepresented in the ranks of research scientists, women who traveled were the first of what became a large and very adventurous contingent. Victorian women were great travelers, and their immediate predecessors resembled them in courage and strength of will. Two cultural practices made travel somewhat easier for women in later decades. First, the Grand Tour was extended to include the whole family. Readers of Charles Dickens's *Little Dorrit* will recall that the novel opens with a number of traveling British families conversing as they wait out quarantine in Marseilles. Second, more intrepid Victorian women often traveled as missionaries, sometimes marrying near-strangers in order to satisfy church regulations that demanded that missionaries journey only in pairs. But in the Romantic period, neither of these was yet a common reason for travel, and the difficulties as well as the adventures were greater. Women who wanted to venture beyond their home turf had to find ways out for themselves, either with a husband or on their own – and, as Lady Hester Stanhope found, it might be easier for a lady to get across the deserts of Syria on her own than to move around London without a carriage.

Lady Hester Stanhope (1776–1839)

Hester Stanhope, like Ada Byron, had a legacy of wealth, breeding, and peculiarity, and while she did not set out to become Queen of the Desert, or a hermit, her strength of will – very different from Ada's – makes her solitary life seem inevitable. Her aristocratic father was famous for his pretensions to democracy. Charles Stanhope's nickname was "Citizen"; he renamed his stately home Democracy Hall, and supported the French Revolution with an enthusiasm that had its equal and opposite in the care he showed for his children, which was almost negligible. There were two sets, three daughters and three sons, from two different marriages. The daughters from the first fared slightly better than the sons, though they were left to governesses who did not make a good impression: "How well I recollect what I was made to suffer when young! and that is the reason why I have sworn eternal warfare against Swiss and French governesses."[28] The girls had been left motherless when Hester, the eldest, was four; the sons were to be raised to be democrats, and taught trades rather than the classics.

It was a deeply unhappy household. Lady Hester left it as a young woman to live with her grandmother, who died not long after Hester's arrival. As a very young woman, she helped her brothers to escape as she had already; the eldest of them had to be spirited away in Citizen Stanhope's absence. She thus found herself early on a social anomaly, a young woman without the protection of a husband or a father. She threw herself on her uncle William Pitt, then Prime Minister and himself famous for his failure to marry. The situation was unusual but happy, and for three years Lady Hester acted as Pitt's hostess at 10 Downing Street. She was here in her element, living in the midst of powerful men – she disliked women – and absorbed in the politics of the day, which she followed with enormous interest.

Pitt, however, died, a martyr to the bottle and the care of his country. After his death Hester Stanhope was left homeless and, for one of her rank, comparatively poor. Her only steady income was a modest government pension. In her view, "a poor gentlewoman is the worst thing in the world," and her liberty of movement was impeded as a poor woman's was not. By her own account, the ultimate reason for Lady Hester's life in the Middle East was that she could not afford a carriage in London. She did not wish to be seen riding in a hackney-coach (the equivalent of a taxi) or even walking with a footman – for she saw so many prostitutes who "flaunt about with a smart footman that I ran the risk of being taken for one of them."[29] Borrowing the carriages of others was feasible only if one could return the favor; and marrying, somehow, was already not the answer she sought. The result was that she felt trapped. Moving to Lebanon is not a solution that would have occurred to everyone, but her original plan was simply to travel to the Middle East and thence, heading east to west, to France, to which the Napoleonic Wars barred entry from the usual ports across the English Channel.

Fate assisted when, in 1811, Lady Hester and her company, traveling in the Levant (an area famous for its pirates, comprising the coastal sections of Turkey, Greece, Egypt, Syria, Lebanon, and what is now Israel), were shipwrecked off Rhodes. The party, which included her maid, her doctor, and her young lover, survived and refitted themselves. Lady Hester adopted the costume she would retain for the rest of her life: men's clothes, Turkish in this first instance. She thus took on – as other women traveling in the Middle East did – a symbolic masculinity and gained the freedom of movement she had not had in London, enforcing the effect by carrying, as well, a brace of pistols, a knife, and a small sword.

Making her way inland, she visited Constantinople, Jerusalem, Jaffa, Palmyra, and Acre, among other cities and settlements, befriending local rulers and attracting crowds, kept safe by her wealth (for here she was wealthy), her generosity, and her daring. She claimed to have been crowned Queen of the Desert (a grand but meaningless title) on her arrival at Palmyra, in the midst of a great procession, in 1813. Nonetheless, she made a great impression on the Bedouins and other tribal groups, and since she was not a colonialist or even a friend to the British consuls in the Middle East, she remained a figure to be admired and, for a long time, turned to for charity.

In 1814 Lady Hester settled in Djoun (or Dar Joun, as the name is sometimes given), on the grounds of a deserted convent given her by the Pasha of Acre. Here, in the Druse Mountains of present-day Lebanon, she built a compound of one-story houses and her "only luxury," a scented garden.[30] And here she spent the rest of her life, never returning to England. She lived as a pasha herself, here where a small fortune went much further than it did in Britain, and where her decisiveness and power of command had much greater scope. Scores of visitors came to see her; she gave charity to the poor ones, practiced astrology and prescribed medicine for everyone, smoking a hookah all the while and, above all, telling stories.

Travel writing is one of the earliest literary genres, and the wish to record one's experience of foreign lands – faithfully or with embellishment – seems the

LADY HESTER STANHOPE.

London Henry Colburn, 1845.

Queen of the Desert

Lady Hester Stanhope spent decades in the desert of present-day Lebanon, living with a freedom she was denied in London. Dressed as a man, she is seen here on horseback and, below, smoking a hookah while conversing with her confidant and doctor, Charles Lewis Meryon; the illustrations are from his Memoirs of the Lady Hester Stanhope, as Related by Herself in Conversations with Her Physician *(London, 1845).* PFORZHEIMER COLLECTION

natural complement of the experience itself. Lady Hester turned the tradition inside out: instead of returning home to tell tales of her life abroad, she created her own small land and told tales of home, talking by the hour of Pitt and other great men she had known in the last days of the eighteenth century. In another sense, she was a throwback to the preliterate traveler since she wrote nothing herself of her stories but depended on her physician, Charles Lewis Meryon, to be her faithful amanuensis. He did not disappoint her, and devoted his later life to the recording of hers. She kept servants by the dozens, since her politics, in precise opposition to her father's, demanded that she maintain her dignity as an aristocrat. The maid and the young lover departed in due time, but in the early years of her life in Djoun, Lady Hester maintained a vigorous correspondence with friends and relatives in Britain.

Lady Hester was a generous hostess, feeding travelers and taking in refugees after the Battle of Navarino in 1827. Slowly, though, the generosity and the fame ebbed as debt undid her, as it had so many other Britons. The moneylenders of the Levant charged, if anything, even higher rates of interest than those in London, and year by year her bills mounted. In 1838 the worst happened when the pension given her on Pitt's death was stopped by the British government because of unpaid debts. Her response was to wall herself into her compound. Charles Meryon was there on a visit, and she sent him off once more to carry the news that she would not leave until it was reinstated. It never was, and when a British diplomat and an American missionary rode out to see how she fared in June of 1839, they found her just dead, lying alone in the compound from which every moveable object had been stolen.

Frances Trollope (1780–1863)

Eleven years earlier, another Englishwoman had come to an almost equally deserted compound a very long way from Djoun. Frances Trollope traveled from London west to Tennessee, to escape (temporarily) an unhappy marriage and to help her friend Frances Wright in developing Nashoba, a utopian community that aimed to educate enslaved Africans in preparation for freedom. Like Lady Hester, she left behind poverty, although hers was not a mere question of being embarrassed to be seen in a hired coach. Frances Trollope had seven children, serious debts, and an attorney husband, Thomas Anthony Trollope, whose bad temper made it impossible for him to retain clients. She set off with her two daughters, her second eldest son, a French artist acquaintance who decided at the last moment to come along, and Frances Wright herself. (Two other sons, Thomas and Anthony, both destined to become novelists – Anthony is still beloved by Anglophiles everywhere – remained at school in England.) Her trip was to result in complete failure in the short term but its story, *Domestic*

Manners of the Americans (1832), was a blazing success, establishing Frances Trollope as a writer and the ugly American as a stereotype.

Trollope's companion, Frances Wright (1795–1852), was a wealthy Scotswoman whose parents had been supporters of the French Revolution; her father distributed Thomas Paine's democratic pamphlets. Wright was orphaned at the age of two and raised by relatives in England with her sister, Camilla. Taking the opposite tack from Lady Hester Stanhope, she laid claim to her radical inheritance with a vengeance. Wright promoted the abolition of established religion, marriage, and slavery, and looked to the United States as the most hopeful place in which to form a new society. She toured the United States with Camilla from 1818 to 1820 and returned for a second journey after writing *Views of Society and Manners in America*. This second trip led Wright to feel, even more strongly than she had after her first, that slavery was the primary evil of American society and that it had to be abolished. Nashoba, a tract of land with a few cabins fifteen miles north of Memphis, was founded as a means to this end.

Intrepid mother
The years of financial stress do not show in this portrait of Frances Trollope. To improve her debt-ridden family's fortunes she sailed to the United States with her friend Frances Wright. Her trip was a failure but her account of it, Domestic Manners of the Americans *(1832), was a blazing success, establishing Trollope as a brilliantly funny writer, and the ugly American as a stereotype.* F. Trollope, *anonymous etching, after a portrait by Auguste Hervieu, ca. 1832.* PRINT COLLECTION

When Trollope and Wright met, the Scotswoman had again returned to England in search of recruits; among others, she sought to induce her friend Mary Shelley to join her. But while Shelley was the daughter of two visionaries and the widow of another, she herself did not feel the need to build the new millennium, and "politely but firmly turned down the invitation."[51] Shelley's instinct was completely correct, at least as far as comfort was concerned. After a voyage up the Mississippi by steamboat that left Frances Trollope declaring that she "would infinitely prefer sharing the apartment of a party of well conditioned pigs" to the gentlemen's lounge with its spit-covered carpet, they arrived, traveling a road cut through forest, at Nashoba.[52] Trollope could only describe it thus: "Desolation was the only feeling – the only word that presented itself; but it was not spoken."[53]

Lost in the American wilderness
The philanthropist Frances Wright founded
Nashoba, in Tennessee, as a utopian commu-
nity to educate slaves in preparation for
freedom. Badly planned, it became a large
mud puddle full of tree stumps and a few
half-finished buildings. Frances Trollope later
described it: "Desolation was the only feeling –
the only word that presented itself." Nashoba
was abandoned, and Wright accompanied the
slaves to their freedom in Haiti. Settlement at
Nashoba, *from Frances Trollope*, Domestic
Manners of the Americans, *3rd ed. (London,*
1832). PFORZHEIMER COLLECTION

Rather disappointingly for readers now, Trollope does not write much more than she spoke, presumably out of consideration for her friend. Nashoba had been promised as a utopian community with a racially integrated school and everything needed for comfortable democratic living. But there had been no progress in its building in Wright's absence, and almost everyone who could leave had left. Its population now consisted of Camilla Wright, Camilla's fiancé, and a small group of slaves, whom prejudice (based on class as much as race) and social difference prevented Trollope from seeing as companions. There was no town nearby; the compound itself consisted of "three roofless cabins in a malaria-ridden swamp."[54] The Trollope group lasted ten days before returning to Memphis. Frances Wright held out for another year, and eventually traveled with the slaves to Haiti, where they were given their freedom and resettled.

However, her departure from Nashoba was far from the end of Trollope's adventures in America. The family moved to the largest nearby city, Cincinnati, where the major business was raising pigs, which ran loose in the streets. They stayed there for two years in the vain hope of getting the son, Henry, set up in some line of business. Henry tried teaching Latin, but the Trollopes found that such things were not called for in the United States – at least, not in Cincinnati. He had considerably more success as a sideshow act called the Invisible Girl; hidden from the audience and speaking in falsetto, he would answer questions in the style of an oracle. But Trollope wished for something more dependable, and opened an ill-fated project called the Bazaar that, with its combination of department store, reading rooms, coffee shops, and stalls for vendors, sounds something like a modern mall. Such emporia had been quite successful in London and might have been in Cincinnati, but the location was badly chosen, Trollope had not made herself particularly well liked, and her husband, entrusted with sending $4,000, sent instead $4,000 worth of unsaleable goods. This was the last straw, and after traveling slowly toward the east coast of the United States, Frances Trollope went home to work her notes up into a book.

She had found plenty to write about. The central theme of *Domestic Manners of the Americans* is that citizens of the United States didn't have any. The men constantly spat, drank whiskey, and talked politics; the women were nonentities barred from public life, whose sole amusement was enthusiastic Christianity. Cincinnati, then on the western edge of the States, was growing rapidly, and the law in frontier towns was toothless. The customs of everyday life (not to call them manners) were a mixture of rudeness and prudery, the latter carried to the extent that the word "shirt" was unspeakable between a young man and young woman. One serious gentleman, vain about his education, told Trollope that "Shakespeare, Madam, is obscene, and, thank God, WE are sufficiently advanced to have found it out!"[55]

This sort of ludicrous judgment was not, perhaps, the worst of the new United States; there was no provision at all, at least in Cincinnati and its environs, for sickness or unemployment. Trollope reported that she had "never seen misery exceed what I have witnessed in an American cottage where disease has entered."[36] Even the minimal assistance offered by the British poor-laws was nonexistent in the United States, and – worse, in Trollope's view – the doctrine of all men (except for enslaved Africans) being equal meant that charitable giving was repugnant, while needing assistance was so shameful that help was accepted with surly ingratitude.

As for women, they were "guarded with a seven-fold shield of habitual insignificance" and barred from public life to a much greater extent than British women. Trollope describes a lecture by Frances Wright in Cincinnati on "the nature of true knowledge," at which, she claims, even her high expectations "fell far short of the splendour, the brilliance, the overwhelming eloquence of this extraordinary orator."[37] For the American audience, however, the wonder was that a woman was speaking at all; and the caricature reproduced here, probably published sometime later, suggests that Wright needed all her courage to continue her tour – as she did, and had her lectures published afterward.

By the time she sat down to write, Frances Trollope had lost all the exalted notions that Wright propounded so magnificently. She returned to England a confirmed Tory and published *Domestic Manners of the Americans* in time to include a preface against the Reform Bill of 1832, which widely expanded the number of voters in Britain. The Reform Bill, happily, we may now say, passed, but Trollope's political loss did no harm to the sales of *Domestic Manners*. The book was an instant bestseller, and while it did not repair the family's fortunes – they moved to Belgium shortly after

A DOWNRIGHT GABBLER, or a goose that deserves to be hissed —

Eloquence
After her utopian project at Nashoba failed, Frances Wright persevered with a speaking tour promoting her ideals; Frances Trollope wrote that even her high expectations were exceeded by "the splendour, the brilliance, the overwhelming eloquence of this extra-ordinary orator." Unfortunately, Wright's lectures sometimes led to caricatures; this one is entitled A Downwright Gabbler, *a pun on her name. Hand-colored lithograph, ca. 1830.* PRINT COLLECTION

to escape their debts, and Thomas Anthony Trollope died there in 1835 – it showed Frances Trollope the way to make a living, and the family eventually made their way back into solvency and comfort.

Trollope went on to write thirty-five novels and five more volumes of travel, sticking to Europe for the latter. None of her later works equalled the success of *Domestic Manners of the Americans*, but she did not disappoint the reputation the book had made for her as a sharp-eyed, honest, and large-hearted observer. In 1843 she joined the English colony of writers in Florence, then a considerably more civilized place than Cincinnati, and died there in 1863.

Maria Dundas Graham, Lady Callcott (1785–1842)

If Frances Trollope may be seen as a forerunner of the sociologist, describing the early life of an American city, Maria Dundas Graham Callcott may be seen as the prototype of an anthropologist. Her books – published under the name Maria Graham – show her taking part, as far as she can, in the lives of those she describes, while Trollope remained a very English woman in the midst of Americans. Graham's immersion in local life means that she is more earnest than Trollope (she is also, simply, not as original a writer), but Graham has the gift of conveying to readers the dignity and interest of people who are very different from them. She sought, in short, to make the British less insular. Both women have, in common with the scientists of the earlier part of this chapter, a facility for taking a deep interest in worlds beyond the self, except that where Caroline Herschel, Anna Atkins, and Ada Byron turned to the natural world, Trollope and Graham turn to the human.

Maria Dundas Graham, later Lady Callcott, was born the daughter of a retired admiral of the Royal Navy, George Dundas. Separated early and unhappily from her mother, she spent most of her youth at school or with relatives. At the age of twenty-three, she sailed to India with her father, going by way of South Africa. She met her first husband, Thomas Graham, another sailor, on the voyage, and never looked back. Until she became an invalid in 1831, she spent much of her life abroad and wrote at least one book for every major voyage she undertook. After 1831, she continued to write from her bed, turning to art history and history for children; her *Little Arthur's History of England* was for many decades a favorite with both children and parents.

Her writings convey the persona of an ideal traveling companion: she is flexible, observant, educated, humorous, and sociable. While there was no need for her to write for money, she had the perseverance required of a professional. Her extraordinary gift for languages must also have been a great convenience to her; after the usual French and less usual Latin at school, she spent her time during her voyage to India in studying Hindi, Chinese, and Persian. Later she added Italian, Spanish, and Portuguese as well as Icelandic (to read the sagas). And while her sketching is not beyond the level of a talented schoolgirl, she was able, with the assistance of professional engravers, to illustrate all of her own books.

Some aspects of India were already well known to Britons, as the imperial place on the Indian subcontinent became more firmly rooted, but Graham sought to make good the lack of a "popular and comprehensive view of its scenery and monuments, and of the manners and habits of its natives and resident colonists."[58] She wrote carefully from her own experience, not hearsay, and though her work was entitled *Journal of a Residence in India*, the original journals were rewritten for a wide readership. Her tolerance of India's religions was looked at askance by some of her more orthodox friends: "She is writing again," one of these wrote to Maria Edgeworth, a mutual friend, "I am sorry to say on heathen Mythology."[59] Italy was an even more familiar destination for British travelers but here, too, Graham's volume filled a gap: the mountains and the campagna surrounding Rome had a reputation somewhat like that of the Wild West in the nineteenth-century United States, and Graham reported to the English for the first time on the peasants who lived there, and the banditti who made life exciting and dangerous for tourists.

South America, however, was terra incognita to most Britons, and Maria Graham's contribution to the knowledge of the world is greatest in her books on Chile and Brazil. Thomas Graham sailed to Chile as the captain of the *Doris*, again looking out for Britain's political interests. Maria Graham clearly loved life at sea; she reminds one of Mrs. Croft, the intrepid admiral's wife in Jane Austen's *Persuasion*, seen in eager conversation with her husband's old naval comrades, the group "forming into a little knot of the navy, Mrs. Croft looking as intelligent and keen as any of the officers around her."[40] Unfortunately, Thomas Graham died during their time abroad. His widow did not return at once, however, and her *Journal of a Voyage to Brazil, and Residence There, During ... 1821, 1822, and 1823* and *Journal of a Residence in Chile During the Year 1822, and a Voyage from Chile to Brazil in 1823* were useful contributions to the current history of those countries, particularly as she arrived in Brazil while the nation was separating from Portugal. Living alone, Maria Graham survived the earthquakes that shook Chile in late 1822 and early 1823, and became briefly, in Brazil, governess to the daughter of the emperor of Brazil.

Graham returned to England to write about her life in South America in two well-received volumes. In 1827 she married an artist named Augustus Wall Callcott, with whom she did not have such exciting destinations as she had before, although it was in his company that she wrote her volume on the mountains near Rome. Lady Callcott – as she became when her second husband was knighted

At home abroad

*Maria Dundas Graham, Lady Callcott wrote at least
one book for every major trip she undertook – to Italy,
South America, and India – and illustrated most of
them herself. This image from her* Journal of a Voyage
to Brazil, and Residence There *(London, 1824) depicts
the mountainous outcropping of rock called Corcovado
("the hunchback") overshadowing Rio de Janeiro,
where Graham (not then Lady Callcott) spent time
as governess to the daughter of the emperor of Brazil.*
RARE BOOKS DIVISION

in 1837 – had suffered intermittently from tuberculosis since childhood, and a ruptured blood vessel left her an invalid in 1831. The last eleven years of her life were spent in London's Kensington, where she is described as making the best of confinement to her bedroom. There, "an immense variety of ... beautiful and sympathetic objects" – prints, paintings, books, and sculptures – were gathered, and a "little bed was placed in a recess, close to a window against which vines had been trained as natural blinds," and among which mice and birds came "half tamed, to take the meals which Lady Callcott daily placed for them."[41] It is an appealing picture of an appealing character, and if she seems all too Victorian in her lingering death, her earlier life, composed of brave adventures and constant writing, distinctly marks her as a citizen of the Romantic era.

Chapter Seven

THE YOUNGEST
ROMANTICS

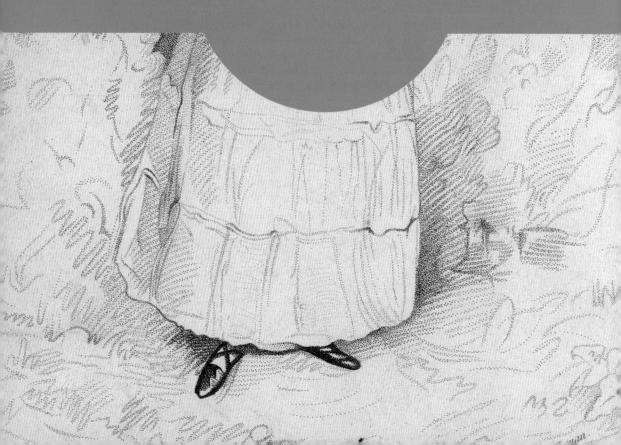

IT WAS CUSTOMARY IN English departments of the mid- and late twentieth centuries to speak of the "older Romantics" – Wordsworth, Coleridge, and sometimes William Blake – and the "younger Romantics" – Shelley (Percy Bysshe, not Mary), Keats, and Byron. This chapter overturns this notion: the four women introduced here – one of them not a writer at all – are *younger* than the "younger Romantics." Coming of age in the later part of the Romantic era, they were formed by it, but like all the women in this book they stand out among that long-skirted, wide-hatted crowd, their peers, their lives giving us a look at the transition from the Romantic to the Victorian period.

Elizabeth
Barrett Browning
(1806–1861)

Elizabeth Barrett Browning seems the embodiment of the Victorian: she looks out from the depths of an engraving (reproduced on the next page) taken from an early photograph, long center-parted ringlets encircling her face in that leonine fashion that took hold in the 1850s, her body draped in a long black dress. And indeed, her story was a Victorian melodrama, in which the invalid heroine elopes secretly with a dashing poet who carries her away from dismal English weather to Italy and sunshine and health, far from the forbidding father who wished none of his children to marry.

The reality, like the Victorian period, was more complex. It is true that in 1846 Elizabeth Barrett and Robert Browning eloped, that her health improved in Italy, and that there was something monstrous about her father. But Elizabeth Barrett Browning was a far more celebrated poet than her husband, and while the change in her personal life was radical, in her professional development the move to Italy simply allowed the full maturing of a life-long vocation. Barrett Browning is extraordinary not only because of her dramatic life but also because she carried on the active life of a professional writer even within the limits of severe ill-health. Moreover, she did so consciously in the footsteps of the Romantic period. Let her speak for herself, in a letter to her friend and fellow-writer Mary Russell Mitford:

I was always insane about books and poems – poems of my own, I mean, – and books of everybody's else – and I read Mary Wolstonecraft when I was thirteen: no, twelve! ... [T]hrough the whole course of my childhood, I had a steady indignation against Nature who made me a woman, and a determinate resolution to dress up in men's clothes as soon as ever I was free of the nursery, and go into the world 'to seek my fortune.' 'How,' was not decided; but I rather leant towards being poor Lord Byron's PAGE.[1]

Byron and Wollstonecraft seem at first a strange pair, but to children of the 1810s and 20s, both were outlaws, dangerous characters, and Elizabeth Barrett took for her Romantic inheritance the right of women to be poets.

Growing up in rural Herefordshire in a fantastic house built by her father, surrounded by a family of eight brothers and three sisters, she lived in a constricted but happy world. Her parents gave her nearly free run of the library and – judging from the title page of "Sebastian, or Virtue Rewarded," an undated effort of earliest youth – they did not suppress her ambition: she identifies "Sebastian" as her "first book" and names herself in childish handwriting as "FRS ASS" and "LLD." To become an associate Fellow of the Royal Society or to become a doctor of laws (as "LLD." implies) was then an impossibility for women, but no one seems to have told Elizabeth Barrett so. She became the family poet early on, writing odes for birthdays and other occasions. The girl's formal education, however, was almost nonexistent; she took learning wherever she could get it, cadging lessons in Greek and Latin from her brother's tutor and later from her brother himself, befriending older men who could teach her still more of the classics.

The Portuguese

Elizabeth Barrett would have looked like this about 1845, when she was writing Sonnets from the Portuguese *for her admirer, the poet Robert Browning, who called her his "Portuguese." They secretly married that year and eloped to Italy.* PFORZHEIMER COLLECTION

Barrett's first volume, privately printed by her parents when she was fourteen, described the Battle of Marathon, fought in 490 B.C.E.; her second was largely an imitation of Alexander Pope, the eighteenth-century master of the heroic couplet; and her third was a translation from Aeschylus, the Greek tragedian. These were all apprentice efforts, and in later poetry Barrett turned resolutely to the present. She could not have known that she was part of the last generation to read poetry in large numbers, but she was determined that hers should speak the language of her time and manners.

After the death of her mother when Elizabeth was twenty-two, the Barretts moved to London, where Edward Moulton Barrett became unwilling to have the family broken up, implicitly forbidding any of the children – now mostly grown – to marry. Most of them lived under the same roof, and Barrett was often confined by illness to her third-floor bed-sitting room. It was here, after a correspondence on literature, that she met Robert Browning. The courtship was concealed not only from her father but from her brothers as well, and the frequency of the post was the lovers' best friend. It was then that Barrett wrote the *Sonnets from the Portuguese*, the love poems by which she is still best known. ("From the Portuguese" is a famous pun: Browning's nickname for her, derived from a poem she wrote honoring the Portuguese poet Luis de Camoẽs, was "the Portuguese," but the phrase also implies that the poems are a translation from the Portuguese tongue.) She and Browning married on September 12, 1846, and left secretly soon after for Italy. The marriage was happy as very few are, and although her father cut her off entirely, Elizabeth Barrett Browning never regretted it. The birth of a son in 1849 was an unlooked-for blessing, and both parents adored and petted him.

Outside of the patriarchal roof, unexpectedly happy, Barrett Browning continued her poetic development. *Aurora Leigh*, nine books and thousands of lines long, is its mature fruit, and an important contribution to the discussion of "the Woman Question" that was carried on in poetry and prose. "Woman questions" is a more accurate way to describe this development of the 1850s, since many were posed: What was the proper place of women? How much education did women need, and for what purpose? Should they have the vote? How was it that middle-class and gentry women were seen as "the angel in the house" while working-class women worked as hard as, and right alongside, equally overworked men, children, and even animals? How was the sexual double

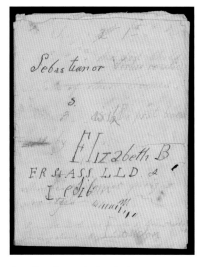

A writer from the beginning
Elizabeth Barrett planned to become a poet, and began working at her craft almost as soon as she could write, as this title page for her first book shows. Her parents, fortunately for her, did not tell her that a girl couldn't become an associate Fellow of the Royal Society, or a doctor of laws (as "FRS ASS" and "LLD." imply). Elizabeth Barrett Browning, "Sebastian, or Virtue Rewarded," autograph manuscript. BERG COLLECTION

standard to be resolved? Barrett Browning's poem addresses many of these concerns. Aurora Leigh, a woman artist, refuses to give up her vocation to marry her cousin-suitor, Romney Leigh. He turns instead to a poor woman, Marian Erle, hoping to bridge the gap between the classes by marrying her, but his plan is derailed after Marian is drugged, raped, and impregnated. She and her child are taken in by Aurora; ultimately, all four end up in Italy.

Barrett Browning's politics are distinctly of her time: very roughly speaking, where the Romantics fought for abstractions – "liberty, equality, fraternity" – the Victorians fought against social problems – child labor, slavery, inadequate education for women. But *Aurora Leigh*'s poetical introspection may owe a debt to Barrett Browning's adult reading in the great Romantic poems of the self – Byron's sardonic epic *Don Juan*, locked up by her father when she was a girl, and Wordsworth's verse autobiography, *The Prelude*, published only in 1850. In its emphasis on the self, *Aurora Leigh* is deeply Romantic.

It was also a great commercial success when it was published in 1857, and sold out its first edition almost immediately. Reviews were mixed, largely on grounds of impropriety: Barrett Browning was proud that some mothers refused to let their daughters read it, and hoped this would make the girls take the poem all the more seriously.[2] Queen Victoria called it "a most extraordinary story and very strange for a woman to have written," while the poet Coventry Patmore wondered that a "modest sensible little woman like Mrs. Browning" could have composed such a thing.[3] But the reading public found it stirring and exciting, and Barrett Browning was satisfied that she had fulfilled the calling of the poet. (Even framing the phrase thus – "the calling of the poet," with its quasi-religious implications – was a Romantic inheritance.) She died of the pulmonary disease that had been with her since adolescence, counting herself a lucky woman, in 1861.

Charlotte Brontë (1816–1855)

Charlotte Brontë's artistic Romantic inheritance came in the form of a wild isolation during childhood. The story of the Brontë family is romantic in the oldest sense of the term: it is a strange tale, stretching the boundaries of belief, so implacably did death run through its members. But some of these early deaths were also the melancholy gifts of the Romantic era, directly attributable to the harsher and more censorious versions of evangelical Protestantism.

First, though, the facts of the matter: Patrick Brontë and Maria Branwell married in Yorkshire in 1812. She was a Cornishwoman, from the temperate maritime southwest of England. He was a Northern Irish Protestant, a clergyman of the Church of England with no income beyond his salary, and when he was offered a permanent position as the parson of Haworth, a Yorkshire village, he took it. The Brontës had six children, born in quick succession between 1814 and 1820: Maria, Elizabeth, Charlotte, Patrick Branwell (called Branwell), Emily, and Anne. Their mother died in 1821, and the children's maternal aunt Elizabeth, respected but not loved, came to stay.

There were serious financial consequences to the death of Maria Brontë, whose small independent income died with her: the five girls would have no marriage portions and would have to make their own ways. Little had changed in women's employment since Mary Wollstonecraft's youth fifty years before, and they were to be educated as governesses. Fortunately – it seemed – for Patrick Brontë, the Clergy Daughters School at Cowan Bridge, further south in Lancashire, had opened in 1823, offering schooling at an affordable rate for just such girls as his, and training them for their careers.

Hannah More made a donation to Cowan Bridge on its opening, but it cannot be said that it was a place after her own heart; she was not a sadist, and girls at Cowan Bridge were cowed, humiliated, and punished for the good of their souls. Nor did the abuse stop at the soul: the horrific descriptions in Charlotte Brontë's *Jane Eyre* of life at Lowood School with its thin uniforms, frozen washbasins, rotten food, and endemic disease are not exaggerations. Maria, Elizabeth, Charlotte, and Emily were all sent to Cowan Bridge in 1824; in 1825, within months of each other, Maria and Elizabeth died of tuberculosis contracted there.

Charlotte and Emily returned, and a long hiatus followed in which they and the others were not sent to school. The village below was not for them – Patrick Brontë did not want his children to mix with the villagers – but the moors with their hills and high skies were open.[4] Human consciousness is highly sensitive to the amount of space allotted to it; wide outdoor spaces impart a sense of liberty. This the surviving Brontë children had in plenty, in common with Wordsworth during his childhood in the greener and more beautiful Lake District to the west. When the sisters began separately to write poetry and novels, the Yorkshire landscape, a gift that most children (girls or boys) simply are not given, stayed with them and nourished them: Charlotte used, as a young teacher, to start off her imagination by remembering the view from her bedroom window at Haworth Parsonage.[5]

If the freedom of the moors was a gift that the Brontë children shared in common with, rather than receiving from, the older Romantics, the populace of their imagination was very much of their own time. Charlotte Brontë in 1829 recorded carefully what newspapers and literary periodicals the family read, noting their politics, and writing about the staff of the leading *Blackwood's Edinburgh Magazine* almost as if they were family themselves: "the editor is Mr Christopher North an old man 74 years of age the 1st of April is his birthday."[6] This awareness of, and wish to take part in, the life of the world outside Haworth shows up in the now-famous games of imagination as well. These began with a set of twelve wooden soldiers that Patrick Brontë gave Branwell, and grew to include a number of different worlds encompassing all the men and women whose doings they knew of from their readings in *Blackwood's* and the newspapers.

The games changed over time, and as she grew older, Charlotte Brontë turned for plots to the annuals, the gift-books full of trite stories for which Letitia Landon and Mary Shelley wrote prolifically. She invented "banal extravaganzas of romantic longing" in which passive women are continually saved by heroic men.[7]

At the same time, the children began to write their stories, with Charlotte the most productive, putting them into tiny illustrated books. All three of the surviving sisters went on to write novels and poetry. Emily Brontë is now seen as the most "Romantic" of the group in the literary sense, making the moors an integral part of her only published novel and inventing in *Wuthering Heights* obsessive loves of the sort she knew only in imagination. She, Branwell, and Anne died within a year of each other, he of alcoholism and the young women of tuberculosis.

All of the Brontës were extraordinary, above all in what now seems their magical and doomed childhood collective. If we remember Charlotte most clearly, it is because she was able to develop her gifts most fully. And unlike Emily, Charlotte became a Victorian, living out conflicts that had been sharpened and defined by the generation before. Hannah More's writings in the 1780s and 90s had encouraged charity school girls to keep in their places, casting broadly a message that others spread as well, until it seemed to some that it was natural for all girls to stay quietly in place. This was never a universal belief, but Charlotte Brontë and many other girls were raised in it, and it had become, by the 1830s and 40s, a stronger presence in the cultural atmosphere than it had been before.

By the time Brontë was writing *Jane Eyre* (published in 1847), her best-known novel, she saw that activity is not the need of men alone. The novel tells the story of an orphan who, having survived a version of Cowan Bridge, becomes a governess and ultimately marries her master. Jane Eyre's happy ending comes only after she discovers at the altar that Mr. Rochester (he has given names – Edward Fairfax – but is constantly referred to as Mr. Rochester) has a wife still living, a madwoman in the attic who is now seen as a symbol of suppressed female energy and anger.[8] However, *Jane Eyre* also speaks openly to the "woman question." Early in her career, Brontë's fierce, plain governess, gaining the open skies on the roof of Thornfield, Mr. Rochester's house, thinks to herself: "It is vain to say human beings ought to be satisfied with tranquillity; they must have action; and they will make it if they cannot find it.... Women are supposed to be very calm generally: but women feel just as men feel; they need exercise for their faculties, and a field for their efforts just as their brothers do."[9]

But where Elizabeth Barrett Browning demanded freedom, Charlotte Brontë's heroine calls for a "field of effort," not a savior or a knight in shining armor. She does not leave her school to seek liberty – for a penniless orphan, Jane tells herself, "such words as Liberty, Excitement, Enjoyment" sound too sweet, are too much to hope for; she asks, rather, for "a new servitude."[10] The demand is distinctly Victorian. Charlotte Brontë shared it with her heroine and made herself an apparently dutiful daughter and – during her brief marriage to her father's assistant – a dutiful wife, combining the two roles by insisting that she and her husband live with her father at Haworth Parsonage. Brontë's passionate nature is striking enough that one biographer has judged it the hallmark of her

A field for their efforts

Charlotte Brontë's life was cut short. She was, however, given more time than her sisters Emily (1818–1848), author of Wuthering Heights *(1848), or Anne (1820–1849), author of* Agnes Grey *(1848) and* The Tenant of Wildfell Hall *(1849), in which to develop her writing. Words from Charlotte's* Jane Eyre *(1847) resonate for all the sisters: "Women are supposed to be very calm generally: but women feel just as men feel; they need exercise for their faculties, and a field for their efforts just as their brothers do." Frontispiece portrait of Charlotte Brontë from Elizabeth Gaskell,* The Life of Charlotte Brontë *(London, 1857).*

PFORZHEIMER COLLECTION

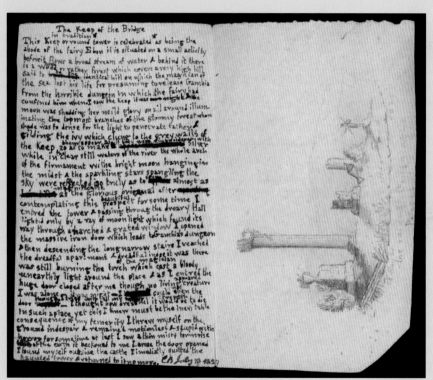

A children's collective

Growing up motherless in an isolated Yorkshire parish, the Brontë children – Anne, Emily, Charlotte, and Branwell – developed a magical and doomed childhood collective, creating entire worlds from their reading and imaginations. (Two other sisters, Maria and Elizabeth, did not survive into adolescence.) Here, in "The Keep of the Bridge" from July 1829, is an example of the tiny books they produced. This one is by Charlotte, shown actual size.

BERG COLLECTION

whole life. However much Brontë's life was populated by Victorian characters and shaped by Victorian institutions, her love of liberty had its roots in the same sources that nourished her Romantic predecessors.[11] Whether or not she would have continued to write in later life is unknowable, since she died nine months after marriage.

However, *Jane Eyre* was not Brontë's only novel, and in *Shirley* (1849) and *Villette* (1853) she continued to explore the possibilities for women's lives. *Villette*, in particular, holds a special place in literature as a novel without resolution. The heroine, Lucy Snowe, is in love with Paul Emanuel, her fellow-teacher at a school based on one where Brontë studied in Brussels. (Like Mary Wollstonecraft's sister Everina, Charlotte and Emily went abroad to learn French.) At the end of the novel he has departed on a dangerous ocean voyage, with the plan of marrying Lucy Snowe on his return. But Brontë entirely frustrates the wishes of her readers to know whether or not he survives, and she even wrote, half-jokingly, to a friend that "Drowning and Matrimony are the fearful alternatives. The merciful .... will of course choose the former and milder doom," while the "cruel-hearted" will insist on "marrying him without ruth or compassion to that – person – that – that – individual – 'Lucy Snowe.'"[12] For Brontë these appellations were no compliment; they meant merely that Lucy Snowe, unattached to anyone else, held little significance in the world. But they also can be applied to Charlotte Brontë herself, who, despite her devotion to duty, had not relinquished the wider vision that let her be an artist as well as a mere individual.

*Queen Victoria
(1819–1901)*

Alexandrina Victoria's Romantic inheritance came early and was soon spent: her mother, the Duchess of Kent, breastfed her daughter, just as Jean-Jacques Rousseau, the Swiss philosopher who was the guiding spirit of European Romanticism, recommended. Generations of children from the middle and upper classes were routinely sent to wet nurses in the first year of their lives. Breastfeeding gradually came to be understood as more natural, more motherly, and better for the child.[13] By the time of Victoria's birth, satires on nursing like James Gillray's *Fashionable Mamma* (see page 160) had become outdated, but the Duchess of Kent was nonetheless the first parent of a British princess to nurse her own child, saying that she would have been desperate "to see my little darling on someone else's breast."[14]

It is unlikely that the Duchess of Kent was consciously following Rousseau's advice; his reputation as a libertine made him a most unlikely model for a mother who was deeply interested in propriety, but Romantic enthusiasm for motherhood was in part his legacy. Victoria's reaction to it was more ambivalent: although domestic life was very important to her as an adult, she disliked babies and, especially, pregnancy, finding that they reminded her too strongly of our being part of the animal world.

Victoria's childhood more strongly evokes – both by its similarities and its differences – another icon of the Romantic era: Princess Charlotte. Victoria's girlhood years are full of echoes of her dead cousin's. Both girls were raised in the expectation that they would be monarchs one day, their lives isolated in royal palaces and far more restricted than those of ordinary children. But where Charlotte had shown herself headstrong, passionately interested in politics, and unwilling to be guided by tutors, Victoria learned early on to depend on order.

Her Little Majesty
Princess Victoria does not look like the sort of girl who would describe herself as "VERY VERY VERY VERY HORRIBLY NAUGHTY!!!!!" – but she did, in 1832, having absorbed a stringent morality. She never grew beyond four feet eleven inches, and the nickname "Her Little Majesty," bestowed by British commoners on their queen, dates from her adulthood. Her Highness the Princess Victoria, *stipple engraving by W. Keenan, undated.* PRINT COLLECTION

Records were kept on her behavior, her daily activities, her studies, her travels, her dolls. As Lynn Vallone observes, writing on Victoria's girlhood and its representations, although the princess was taught – as Hannah More recommended – to love truth, it is more accurate to say that she "loved precision in all things."[15] Overseen by her beloved governess, the Baroness Lehzen, she tracked herself in the daily entries of the "Good Behaviour Books" from about the age of twelve. Although she was not informed officially that she was next in line to the throne until she was eleven, she had intimations of her position earlier, and began by ruling herself. She was a harsh judge, recording one day, for instance, that she had been "VERY VERY VERY VERY HORRIBLY NAUGHTY!!!!!"[16]

Vallone speculates that the princess may have been raised according to Hannah More's *Hints Towards Forming the Character of a Young Princess*, the conduct book so despised by its original audience.[17] Her upbringing was sheltered well into her adolescence, according to the plan of her mother's adviser Sir John Conroy, an ambitious man whom Victoria came to loathe. More's influence, emphasizing Christian morality and humility, was benign in comparison. Certainly Victoria's academic studies follow, generally, More's recommendations; they included Latin,

The Fashionable Mamma, —or— The Convenience of Modern Dress. *Vide, The Pocket Hole, &c.*

The Romantic way to feed a baby

One of the Princess Victoria's few direct legacies from the Romantic period was that she was breastfed by her mother. For preceding generations it had been traditional to hire a wet nurse. But the Swiss philosopher Jean-Jacques Rousseau encouraged women to "follow nature," and the practice became fashionable, then widespread. James Gillray's The Fashionable Mamma, or The Convenience of Modern Dress *(1796), made before Victoria's birth, also mocks rich women who were not going to allow maternal duties to stand in the way of fashion.*

PRINT COLLECTION

*Queen Victoria's drawing. Presented to M.V.C. —
by Mr Chambers, who received it from Mr Westall
the Queen's tutor, when she was Princess. —*
CCClarke
Sepr 1838

*Contributed to the Album of Victoria Beatrice Gigliucci for her Birthday
on the 13th May 1886 by her loving Grand=Aunt*
Mary Victoria Cowden=Clarke .

A royal hand
*Princess Victoria's lessons, like those of most
genteel girls, included drawing, for which
she showed a marked talent. This pencil
sketch, ca. 1824, was later donated by her old
teacher to a charitable cause.* PFORZHEIMER
COLLECTION

French, German, history, arithmetic, "poetry by heart," and drawing. On becoming queen, a month after her eighteenth birthday, Victoria dismissed Conroy, an action that might be read as Romantic insistence on liberty, or as a Hannah More–like assertion of correct action, or simply as the natural result of being released from a painful confinement.

While her place as an extraordinary woman on the verge of the era named for her is undeniable, Victoria's lifetime achievement consists largely in her longevity and ability to adapt as the political power of the crown diminished steadily over her long reign. From her husband, Albert, she learned to be a firm Tory and a loving wife. Victoria grew ever more interested in Britain's empire, taking Hindustani lessons and, in 1876, delighting in the addition of the title Empress of India to that of Queen, seeing that empire was an unalloyed good. (Millions of Indians saw the matter rather differently.) She built a model of monarchy that took in all the virtues of the middle class – conventionality, truthfulness, the wish to be good – and made them royal as well. The child who saw herself as so very naughty grew up to an unimpeachable morality, steadying the British monarchy and, to some extent, the nation as well, by her great moral weight.

George Eliot (1819–1880)

Judged by her writing, George Eliot is one of the least Romantic of the writers discussed in this book. But if her writing – realistic, expansive, concrete, deeply thoughtful – is not "Romantic," the events of her life in many ways recapitulate those of the period and take them a few steps further into the future. She was born Mary Ann Evans in Warwickshire, in the quiet countryside that she loved and that formed the primary geography for her novels. Her schooling, while conventional, was supplemented and extended through her whole life by her enormously receptive mind. She became an evangelical Christian in her early teens, maintaining a standard of piety that left her classmates bemused. Evans's hunger for learning led her to theology, and she began to meet and befriend skeptics, both in print and in person. Gradually but decisively she lost the faith of her girlhood, and in 1842 she stopped going to church. Now calling herself by the more urbane name of Marian Evans, she became a prototype of that most Victorian character, the man or woman who has lost religion without losing the religious sensibility, the moral seriousness that is at the core of her life and work.

After her father's death in 1849, Marian Evans began to carry out her own sexual revolution. She began by establishing a place and then a name for herself in the London literary world. She moved to the city, and, through a largely anonymous literary apprenticeship in editing, translating, and writing essays and book reviews, transformed herself into a consummate professional. When Evans saw that she had a vocation for fiction, she signed herself George Eliot. Eliot chose pseudonymity primarily because she did not wish her books to be judged by the easy standards allowed to "Silly Novels by Lady Novelists," to use the title of one of her own essays. Beyond this, there was another reason: by 1856, when she began writing fiction, Eliot was living with George Henry Lewes, the man she loved and referred to as her husband, but to whom she was not, and would never be, married.

Why hide behind the pseudonym? Mary Wollstonecraft had done no such thing: all of her most important works appeared under her own name. But Wollstonecraft did pretend that she was married to Gilbert Imlay, while Eliot, among her friends and acquaintances, did no such thing. It is not that Eliot had nothing to fear from both friends and strangers; on the contrary, she paid heavily for her decision in social ostracism. But Eliot had three advantages that Mary Wollstonecraft lacked. First, despite being barred from wider society, she nonetheless had a larger social circle than Wollstonecraft had had. She and Lewes were not the only man and woman who lived as they did. Their circle included Lewes's legal wife, who had four children by Thornton Hunt, the son of a great friend of Percy Bysshe Shelley's, and whose decisions had been based, in part, on Shelley's example and thought. What's more, the romantic and domestic pleasures of her life with Lewes were considerable: Wollstonecraft too had met her match, but George Eliot was given years of partnership, as her predecessor had not been, with a man who encouraged in every way her work in literature.

Revolutions in her lifetime

Born Mary Ann Evans, George Eliot renamed herself when she began to write fiction, adopting the first name of her companion, George Henry Lewes, who was legally tied to another woman. Though her novels – realistic, expansive, witty, deeply thought-ful – are not "Romantic," the sexual and religious revolutions that she experienced in her life recapitulated those of the Romantic period and took them a few steps into the future. Etching by P. Rajon, after F. W. Burton, before 1875. PRINT COLLECTION

Second, she was not isolated polit-ically, in that there was a women's movement already in existence. The "woman question" – or questions – that occupied Elizabeth Barrett Browning were also concerns for Eliot, and many of her friends were women who supported these causes, in particular Barbara Leigh Smith Bodichon, who left her fortune to Girton College, the first Cambridge college for women. Finally, Eliot was not isolated historically. She had the example of Mary Wollstonecraft before her and she valued her predecessor, whose reputation was still slightly dubious. Eliot wrote in an 1855 review titled "Margaret Fuller and Mary Wollstonecraft" that "[t]here is in some quarters a vague prejudice against the *Rights of Woman* as in some way or other a reprehensible book, but readers who go to it with this impression will be surprised to find it eminently serious, severely moral, and withal rather heavy – the true reason, perhaps, that no edition has been published since 1796, and that it is now rather scarce."[18] Despite its heaviness, Eliot sees her predecessor's *Vindication of the Rights of Woman* as comparing favorably with Fuller's *Woman in the Nineteenth Century*.

But neither Eliot nor Elizabeth Barrett Browning, after her girlhood enthusiasm, was an outright supporter of women's rights. Wollstonecraft was a valued predecessor but not an intellectual model. Eliot wrote in a letter, years after the review of Margaret Fuller's book, that "[t]here is no subject on which I am more inclined to hold my peace and learn, than on the 'Woman Question.' ... Conclusions seem easy so long as we keep large blinkers on and look in the direction of our own private path."[19] Eliot was too much an artist to be willing to sacrifice herself to the unitary point of view that political debate demands. Wollstonecraft loved a good fight, but Eliot, although she went about it in an unconventional and courageous way, strove for a quiet domestic life. She knew, however, that Wollstonecraft's work had a share in clearing her private path. Eliot's novels – the best known of which are *The Mill on the Floss* (1860), *Middlemarch* (1871), and *Daniel Deronda* (1876) – are thoroughly Victorian in their attention to the details of daily life and penetration of moral vision. But while these are exemplary of the mid-Victorian period, they are equally, along with Eliot's ironic humor, gifts of her own extraordinary mind, which could mature only after she had relived religious and sexual struggles of the Romantic era.

Social movements demanding improvements in the lives of British women grew up in the decades immediately following Victoria's coronation, led by both women and men. Some of the women who have been described here would have been appalled by the changes proposed in the 1850s and 60s: university education, the vote, equality in law with men, custodial rights to children – these were all revolutionary proposals in the 1790s, and yet many of them had been realized before the end of Victoria's reign.

The women who would have fought these changes tooth and nail now seem furthest from us. These women embodied and worked to preserve, as Felicia Hemans, Queen Victoria, and Hannah More did, the particular values of their social class, place, and time. Their extraordinariness comes from their powerful articulation of those values, even though these may no longer seem useful to us. It hardly seems now like a good idea that servant girls should be ignorant of the art of writing, for instance: near-universal literacy in the West has gone a great way to make the job of servant girl obsolete, even as it has given new life to those of cleaning lady and nanny. Even more remote are the women who lived solitary or nearly solitary lives – Hester Stanhope in her desert stronghold, Eleanor Butler and Sarah Ponsonby in their cottage at Llangollen. These women are extraordinary because of their singularity, and while they fascinate, the resonance of their lives has a fairy-tale feeling to it, as it did in their own lifetimes. The women in this book with the most enduring strength of mind are those who spoke both to their generations and ours. These – like Jane Austen, George Eliot, and Mary Wollstonecraft – thought and lived wholly within the problems and demands of their own time, but left us with thoughts that defy, even if briefly, the distance between us and them.

Room 319 at The New York Public Library –
the home and reading room of the
Pforzheimer Collection – as it is today,
with many of the antique furnishings from
the original collector's library.

THE PFORZHEIMER COLLECTION AND
ITS FEMALE INHABITANTS: AN AFTERWORD

Stephen Wagner

Dating back to the years after World War I – a time when many large private libraries were being dispersed – the Carl H. Pforzheimer Collection of Shelley and His Circle at The New York Public Library is one of the world's leading repositories for the study of English Romanticism. The creation of Carl H. Pforzheimer (1879–1957), who brought to the world of books and manuscripts the same shrewdness and determination that had already made him the country's most prominent dealer in oil securities, the collection now comprises some 25,000 items, including books, manuscripts, letters, and other objects, chiefly from the late eighteenth and early nineteenth centuries.

Pforzheimer's taste was eclectic and wide-ranging. Eventually his library came to include early printing, illuminated manuscripts, Elizabethan and Jacobean literature, children's books, and American historical documents – not to mention that Holy Grail of book collecting, a Gutenberg Bible. But it was the lives and work of the English Romantics that most caught his imagination, preoccupying him for the last two decades of his life. He had started to collect Shelley material in 1920 when an extraordinary trove of material once owned by the scholar, bibliophile, and forger H. Buxton Forman appeared on the market. This purchase served to ignite a consuming passion – to build a collection that would document the lives of a small circle of remarkably talented writers who flourished in England during the decades following the French Revolution: the poet Percy Bysshe Shelley, his wife Mary Shelley, her father and mother, William Godwin and Mary Wollstonecraft, and a circle of friends that included Lord Byron, Leigh Hunt, Thomas Love Peacock, and Edward John Trelawny.

Pforzheimer's interests took him far beyond the usual highlights that most collectors fixate on, however, for in addition to the customary first editions and canonical literary manuscripts, he sought out other kinds of material: deeds, wills, tradesmen's bills, promissory notes, insurance policies, and above all correspondence – the letters that linked parents and children, husbands and wives, writers and publishers, friends, lovers, and enemies. Moreover, as his obsession grew, it soon became evident that each figure in the "circle" would spawn another circle, and that by pursuing these secondary or tertiary orbiting figures, he would soon build a collection encompassing the entire range of literary activity in Britain during the Romantic period. At the same time, driven by the desire to provide a context for the literary works, Pforzheimer's collecting goals broadened further to include political and scientific treatises, contemporary travel guides and road books, diaries and commonplace books, grammars and dictionaries, almanacs and business directories, as well as a wide assemblage of topical pamphlets, broadsides, chapbooks, prints, and other ephemera. As a result, the current collection supports research not only in literary studies but also in social, political, and cultural history and – not least – women's studies.

There is a certain irony in the fact that such a collection, inspired by and initially focused upon the work of a canonical male writer such as Shelley, should have evolved into a major archive of writings by and about women. The responsibility lies entirely with Shelley. When he seduced the sixteen-year-old daughter of his mentor, the anarchist philosopher William Godwin – courting her literally on her mother's grave – his life and literary reputation became inextricably bound up with what is arguably the most formidable mother-daughter combination that ever put pen to paper: the mother, author of the founding text of modern feminism, *A Vindication of the Rights of Woman*; the daughter, not yet out of her teens, trying to come up with a ghost story "as good as the boys' " (the boys, in this case, being Byron and Shelley) and, in so doing, formulating the prevailing cultural myth not just for the remainder of her century, but for the one that followed, and – if its end turns out at all like its beginning – for the current one as well. The story, of course, is *Frankenstein*, that definitive statement regarding the law of unintended consequences. And from these two figures – Mary Wollstonecraft in the late eighteenth century, and Mary Shelley in the first half of the nineteenth – no more than one or two of the allowable "six degrees of separation" are needed to establish a connection with virtually every woman writer and intellectual of the time.

Accordingly, the Pforzheimer's manuscript holdings feature in depth such figures as Lady Blessington, Claire Clairmont, Mary Hays, Felicia Hemans, Lady Mount Cashell, Caroline Norton, Amelia Opie, and Jane Porter, as well as what amounts to a small archive in its own right devoted to the galaxy of women surrounding Lord Byron – his mother, wife, daughter, half sister, and various mistresses, including an extensive array of letters by his "last attachment," the Countess Teresa Guiccioli. This material is supplemented by scattered holdings relating to such figures as Joanna Baillie, Charlotte Bury, Maria Edgeworth, Catharine Macaulay, Harriet Martineau, Lady Morgan, Mary Robinson, Anna Seward, Frances Trollope, and Helen Maria Williams, along with a handful of iconic literary manuscripts by such post-Romantic icons as Charlotte Brontë, Elizabeth Barrett Browning, and George Eliot. Rounded out with a broad array of contemporary printed materials, the collection might be said to illuminate the entire range of women's activities in Great Britain during its time frame.

In 1957, following his death, the collections of Carl Pforzheimer became an asset of The Carl and Lily Pforzheimer Foundation, Inc. While the non-Romantic portions were gradually sold or given away, his Shelley collection continued to grow, and its holdings of women authors expanded commensurately. Key acquisitions during this period included the Guiccioli-Gamba papers, the Mount Cashell–Cini papers, and the correspondence of Mary Hays. However, it had always been Carl Pforzheimer's intention that his favorite offspring would in time become part of a public institution. In 1986 this final wish was realized when the Foundation presented the Carl H. Pforzheimer Collection of Shelley and His Circle to The New York Public Library – a gift underwritten by a generous endowment that allows for its conservation and future growth.

But how was it to grow? By the time it came to NYPL, the collection could lay claim to early printings of all the major Romantic texts – with one or two exceptions so rare as to be unobtainable – and most of the minor ones. Moreover, manuscripts from this period surface only infrequently (for example, two Mary Wollstonecraft letters in the last thirty years). A solution was to return to the founder's original vision: the lives *and* the times, with a renewed emphasis on the times. Topics such as early radicalism (and its conservative counterpart), English responses to the French Revolution, publishing history, travel, social reform, science and technology, are now pursued almost as aggressively as literature. And as the canon has expanded its membership rolls, writings by and about women receive special consideration. Conduct books and treatises on beauty, domestic economy, etiquette, and female education; trials for adultery and rape; books on travel, science, and religion by women writers; feminist, proto-feminist, and anti-feminist tracts; keepsake albums and commonplace books; all these, as well as books and manuscripts by female authors of the period, both major and minor, are sought out.

As these lines are being written, the day's mail is delivered to the Pforzheimer Collection: a package containing letters written by Queen Caroline, Caroline Herschel, and Lady Hester Stanhope; and another with two books: *The Lady's Toilette; containing a critical examination of the nature of beauty, and of the causes by which it is impaired: with instructions for preserving it to advanced age; an historical sketch of the fashions of France and England, directions for dressing with taste and elegance; and receipts for preparing all the best and most harmless cosmetics proper for a lady's use* (London: printed for W. H. Wyatt, 1808) and Maria Charlesworth's *The Female Visitor to the Poor: or records of female parochial visiting. By a clergyman's daughter* (London: Seeley, Burnside, and Seeley, 1846). These have all now become typical acquisitions. Shelley, who had great admiration for women's minds, is no longer quite at the exact center of the circle. Somehow, one suspects he wouldn't have minded at all.

NOTES

FOREWORD

1 More widely available through the ten volumes of *Shelley and his Circle* with their authoritative commentaries.

PREFACE

1 Mary Wollstonecraft, *Letters Written During a Short Residence in Sweden, Norway, and Denmark* [1796], ed. Richard Holmes (Harmondsworth: Penguin Books, 1987), 97.

CHAPTER ONE.
MARY ROBINSON,
EIGHTEENTH-CENTURY ROMANTIC

1 There is some question about Robinson's birthdate but it is clear that the one she gives in her memoirs, 1758, is false; 1757 is likelier. See Paula Byrne, "A Maniac for Perdita," *TLS*, August 6, 2004, or Byrne's forthcoming biography of Mary Robinson.

2 William Wordsworth, *The Prelude* (1805 version), Book X, lines 693–94.

3 *The Longman Handbook of Modern British History, 1714–1995*, 3rd ed., ed. Chris Cook and John Stevenson (London: Longman, 1996), 151.

4 The first use recorded in the *Oxford English Dictionary* of "middle class" as a singular noun prefixed by "the," rather than the adjectival "middling class," or plural "middle classes," dates to 1792; the source is the second part of Thomas Paine's *Rights of Man.*

5 Byrne, "A Maniac for Perdita."

6 Laetitia Mathilda Hawkins, *Memoirs*, 2: 24, quoted in the *Dictionary of National Biography*, s.v. Mary Robinson.

7 The existence of another actress who also went by "Mrs. Robinson" has made the precise date of Mary Robinson's retirement from the stage a matter of minor controversy.

8 Charlotte Smith, preface to the 6th ed. of her *Elegiac Sonnets*; quoted in Jacqueline Labbe, "Selling One's Sorrows: Charlotte Smith, Mary Robinson, and the Marketing of Poetry," *Wordsworth Circle* 25, no. 2 (Spring 1994): 68.

9 Robert D. Bass, *The Green Dragoon: The Lives of Banastre Tarleton and Mary Robinson* (New York: Henry Holt, 1957), 381, 398.

10 See Stuart Curran, "Mary Robinson's *Lyrical Tales* in Context," in *Re-Visioning Romanticism*, ed. Carol Shiner Wilson and Joel Haefner (Philadelphia: University of Pennsylvania Press, 1994), 21.

11 Wordsworth, *The Prelude* (1805 version), Book XI, lines 308–11.

12 Coleridge to Robert Southey, January 25, 1800; *Collected Letters of Samuel Taylor Coleridge*, ed. Earl Leslie Griggs (Oxford: Clarendon Press, 1956), 562; ampersands have been expanded to "and."

CHAPTER TWO.
EXEMPLARY WOMEN:
MARY WOLLSTONECRAFT, HANNAH MORE, AND THEIR WORLDS

1 Anne Stott's *Hannah More: The First Victorian* (Oxford: Oxford University Press, 2003) is the standard biography of More. My account of More leans heavily on Stott's work.

2 See, for instance, Anne K. Mellor, *Mothers of the Nation: Women's Political Writing in England, 1780–1830* (Bloomington: Indiana University Press, 2000), 18–19.

3 Virginia Woolf, "Mary Wollstonecraft," *The Common Reader, Second Series* (New York: Alfred A. Knopf, 1948), 176.

4 More in a letter of 1783; quoted in Stott, *Hannah More*, 6.

5 Janet Todd, *Mary Wollstonecraft: A Revolutionary Life* (New York: Columbia University Press, 2000), 56.

6 Wollstonecraft to Henry Gabell, September 13, 1787; *Collected Letters of Mary Wollstonecraft*, ed. Ralph M. Wardle (Ithaca, N.Y.: Cornell University Press, 1979), 161.

7 Stott, *Hannah More*, i.

8 *Shelley and his Circle*, ed. Doucet Devin Fischer and Donald H. Reiman (Cambridge, Mass.: Harvard University Press, 1961–), 9: 1–24.

9 Mary Wollstonecraft, *A Vindication of the Rights of Woman* [1792], ed. Carol Poston (New York: W. W. Norton, 1975), 45.

10 Quoted from *The Life of William Wilberforce*, 1: 149, in Stott, *Hannah More*, 95.

11 Hannah More, *Coelebs in Search of a Wife* [1808] (New York: Harper and Brothers, 1855), 327.

12 Hannah More, *Strictures on the Modern System of Female Education; with a View of the Principles and Conduct Prevalent Among Women of Rank and Fortune*, in *The Complete Works of Hannah More* (New York: Harper and Brothers, 1836), 7.

13 More, *Strictures*, 2: 27, quoted in Stott, *Hannah More*, 221.

14 More, *Strictures*, 45.

15 Lines 63–64, quoted in Stott, *Hannah More*, 93.

16 Wollstonecraft, *A Vindication of the Rights of Woman*, ed. Poston, 9.

17 Virginia Woolf, "Mary Wollstonecraft," 176.

18 William Godwin, from *Memoirs of the Author of A Vindication of the Rights of Woman* (1798), quoted in the prefatory note to *Letters Written During a Short Residence in Norway, Sweden, and Denmark*, in *The Works of Mary Wollstonecraft*, ed. Janet Todd and Marilyn Butler (New York: New York University Press, 1989), 6: 238.

19 Wollstonecraft to Godwin, June 6, 1797; *Collected Letters of Mary Wollstonecraft*, 396.

20 Stott, *Hannah More*, 274; "rational delight" is from the novel's epigraph and comes from *Paradise Lost*.

CHAPTER THREE.
NOT QUITE GOOD ENOUGH:
THREE IMPERFECT LIVES

1 Hannah More, *Hints Towards Forming the Character of a Young Princess*, 3rd ed. (London: Cadell and Davies, 1805), 1: 17.

2 Stott, *Hannah More*, 261.

3 *Letters of the Princess Charlotte, 1811–1817*, ed. A. Aspinall (London: Home and Van Thal, 1949), 38.

4 Quoted in Christopher Hibbert, *George IV: Regent and King* (London: Allen Lane, 1973), 4.

5 Quoted in Alison Plowden, *Caroline and Charlotte: The Regent's Wife and Daughter, 1795–1821* (London: Sidgwick & Jackson, 1989), 95.

6 Plowden, *Caroline and Charlotte*, 20.

7 Plowden, *Caroline and Charlotte*, 69.

8 Plowden, *Caroline and Charlotte*, 87.

9 Aspinall, ed., *Letters of the Princess Charlotte*, xii. The picture in question was said to have been a caricature of Emma, Lady Hamilton (see Chapter Four).

10 Mary Wollstonecraft, *A Vindication of the Rights of Woman* [1792] (London: Penguin, 1992), 233.

11 Plowden, *Caroline and Charlotte*, 100, quoting from a letter of December 20, 1811.

12 Stephen C. Behrendt, *Royal Mourning and Regency Culture: Elegies and Memorials of Princess Charlotte* (New York: St. Martin's Press, 1997), 38.

13 Margaret King Moore, "Lettera a Sua Figlie" ("Letter to Her Daughters"), autograph manuscript in the Carl H. Pforzheimer Collection of Shelley and His Circle, The New York Public Library, Astor, Lenox and Tilden Foundations, 1. There is some question over her date of birth; her most recent biographer, Janet Todd, thinks 1771 is most likely. See *Rebel Daughters: Ireland in Conflict 1798* (New York: Viking, 2003), 20 and 341n.

14 Moore, "Lettera a Sua Figlie," 2.

15 Margaret King Moore, *Advice to Young Mothers on the Physical Education of Children* (London: Longman, Hurst, Rees, Orme and Brown, 1823), 172–73.

16 Edwin McAleer, *The Sensitive Plant: A Life of Lady Mount Cashell* (Chapel Hill: University of North Carolina Press, 1958), 147, quoting from Claire Clairmont.

17 Moore, "Lettera a Sua Figlie," 4.

18 Moore, "Lettera a Sua Figlie," 5.

19 Quoted in Alan Chedzoy, *A Scandalous Woman: The Story of Caroline Norton* (London: Allison and Busby, 1992), 60.

20 *The Crim. Con. Gazette*, November 10, 1858, 1.

21 See Jane Gray Perkins, *The Life of Mrs. Norton* (London: John Murray, 1909), 140.

22 See Perkins, *The Life of Mrs. Norton,* 44–45.

CHAPTER FOUR.
THE MODERN VENUS, OR,
IMPROPER LADIES AND OTHERS

1 Gillian Russell, "'Faro's Daughters': Female Gamesters, Politics, and the Discourse of Finance in 1790s Britain," *Eighteenth-Century Studies* 33, no. 4 (Summer 2000): 481.

2 Amanda Foreman, *Georgiana, Duchess of Devonshire* (New York: Random House, 1998), 178 ff.; Foreman gives the figure of £6 million, which I have translated conservatively into dollars.

3 See Russell, "'Faro's Daughters,'" 486 and 501n22.

4 On women's participation in elections, see Elaine Chalus, "Women, Electoral Privilege and Practice in the Eighteenth Century," in *Women in British Politics, 1760–1860: The Power of the Petticoat*, ed. Kathryn Gleadle and Sarah Richardson (Houndmills, Basingstoke: Macmillan, 2000), and Judith S. Lewis, "1784 and All That," in *Women, Privilege, and Power: British Politics, 1750 to the Present*, ed. Amanda Vickery (Stanford, Calif.: Stanford University Press, 2001). See also Renata Lana, "Women and Foxite Strategy in the Westminster Election of 1784," *Eighteenth-Century Life* 26, no. 1 (2002): 46–69.

5 Quoted in Stott, *Hannah More*, 66.

6 For the classic exposition of this view, see Lawrence Stone, *The Family, Sex and Marriage in England 1500–1800* (New York: Harper and Row, 1977).

7 Information on the Duchess of Devonshire is based on Amanda Foreman's *Georgiana, Duchess of Devonshire*.

8 Anna Clark, "Queen Caroline and Sexual Politics," in *Scandal: The Sexual Politics of the British Constitution* (Princeton: Princeton University Press, 2004), 199–201.

9 On the symbolic aspects of Queen Caroline's "trial" and death see, besides Plowden and Clark, Flora Fraser, *The Unruly Queen: The Life of Queen Caroline* (London: Macmillan, 1996).

10 Material on Harriet Shelley is taken from Kenneth Neill Cameron, "The Last Days of Harriet Shelley," in *Shelley and his Circle*, 4: 774.

11 *Shelley and his Circle*, 4: 774.

12 *Shelley and his Circle*, 4: 778.

13 *Shelley and his Circle*, 4: 805.

14 On the publication of the *Memoirs* see Frances Wilson, *The Courtesan's Revenge: Harriette Wilson, the Woman Who Blackmailed the King* (London: Faber, 2003), chapters 19–21.

15 Wilson, *The Courtesan's Revenge*, 225.

16 Wilson, *The Courtesan's Revenge*, 198.

17 Harriette Wilson, *Memoirs* [1825] (London: Peter Davies, 1929), 1.

18 Granville Leveson-Gower, quoted in Flora Fraser, *Emma, Lady Hamilton* (New York: Knopf, 1987), 276.

19 See Fraser, *Emma, Lady Hamilton*, 313.

20 Shearer West, "The Public and Private Roles of Sarah Siddons," in *A Passion for Performance: Sarah Siddons and Her Portraitists*, ed. Robyn Asleson (Los Angeles: J. Paul Getty Museum, 1999), 5.

21 Quoted in Claire Tomalin's excellent *Mrs. Jordan's Profession: The Story of a Great Actress and a Future King* (New York: Viking, 1994), 245, from a letter of November 1811 to Mercer Elphinstone. I have expanded a contraction.

22 Quoted in Tomalin, *Mrs. Jordan's Profession*, 268.

23 The still-standard work on lesbian history in this period is Emma Donoghue's *Passions Between Women: British Lesbian Culture 1688–1801* (London: Scarlet Press, 1993).

24 For the most complete coverage of this custom, see Rudolf Dekker and Lotte van de Pol, *The Tradition of Female Transvestism in Early Modern Europe* (Basingstoke: Macmillan, 1989).

25 Emma Donoghue found this extraordinary statistic in Sheridan Baker, "Henry Fielding's *Female Husband*," *PMLA* 74 (June 1959): 224; she quotes it in *Passions Between Women*, 74.

26 Baker, "Henry Fielding's *Female Husband*," 213.

27 The double "l" is flapped with the tongue; the easiest way to approximate the sound is to pronounce it with an "h" before the "l."

28 Journal paraphrased in Elizabeth Mavor, *The Ladies of Llangollen: A Study in Romantic Friendship* (Harmondsworth, Middlesex: Penguin, 1971), 57.

29 This and the previous quotation from Hester Thrale Piozzi are from Donoghue, *Passions Between Women*, 150.

CHAPTER FIVE.
STRONGER PASSIONS OF THE MIND:
WOMEN IN LITERATURE AND
THE VISUAL ARTS

1 Cynthia Lawford is the discoverer of the story and the author of a biography of Letitia Elizabeth Landon, not yet published at the time of this writing. For a brief version of the story, and Lawford's consideration of how the knowledge of Landon's history might change the way we read her work, see "'Thou shalt bid thy fair hands rove': L. E. L.'s Wooing of Sex, Death and the Editor," in *Romanticism on the Net*, Issues 29–30, February–May 2003. URL: <http://www.erudit.org/revue/ron/2003/v/n29/007718ar.html>

2 Lawford, "'Thou shalt bid thy fair hands rove...,'" paragraph 21.

3 Lawford, "'Thou shalt bid thy fair hands rove...,'" paragraph 20.

4 See Lawford, "'Thou shalt bid thy fair hands rove...,'" paragraph 10.

5 Canto I, stanza 194, lines 1–2.

6 Quoted without source in the *Dictionary of National Biography*.

7 Quoted in E. J. Clery, *Women's Gothic from Clara Reeve to Mary Shelley* (Tavistock: Northcote House in association with the British Council, 2000), 85.

8 See Ellen Donkin, *Getting into the Act: Women Playwrights in London, 1776–1829* (London: Routledge, 1994), 170–72.

9 *Dublin University Magazine* 37 (April 1851): 529; quoted in Paula Feldman, ed., *British Women Poets of the Romantic Era* (Baltimore: Johns Hopkins University Press, 1997), 23.

10 Nora Nachumi, conversation, September 14, 2004.

11 Jane Austen, *Northanger Abbey* [1817], ed. Claire Grogan (Peterboro, Ont.: Broadview, 1996), 60.

12 The episode and more may be found in *The Education of the Heart: The Correspondence of Rachel Mordecai Lazarus and Maria Edgeworth*, ed. Edgar E. MacDonald (Chapel Hill: University of North Carolina Press, 1977).

13 *Jane Austen's Letters*, ed. Deirdre Le Faye, 3rd ed. (Oxford: Oxford University Press, 1995), 275.

14 See Rictor Norton, *The Mistress of Udolpho: A Biography of Ann Radcliffe* (Leicester: University of Leicester Press, 1999), 220–21.

15 Mary Shelley, Introduction to the 1831 edition of *Frankenstein*; cited from *Frankenstein, or the Modern Prometheus*, ed. Susan Wolfson (New York: Longman, 2003), 189.

16 Shelley, *Frankenstein*, 191.

17 Quoted from a letter to Charles Lamb, ca. 1808, in Katharine Anthony, *The Lambs: A Story of Pre-Victorian England* (New York: Alfred A. Knopf, 1945), 95.

18 Peter Rowland, letter, *TLS*, December 9, 2003, 17.

19 Austen, *Northanger Abbey*, 125.

20 The positioning of Kauffmann and Moser in Zoffany's picture is pointed out by Whitney Chadwick in *Women, Art and Society*, 3rd ed. (London: Thames and Hudson, 2002), 7.

21 The account of Lady Diana Beauclerk's life that follows is drawn from Carola Hicks's engaging biography, *Improper Pursuits: The Scandalous Life of Lady Di Beauclerk* (London: Macmillan, 2001).

22 Correctly pronounced, the last two-thirds of this name will sound as though spelled "Sinjun Bullingbrook."

23 Hicks, *Improper Pursuits*, 247.

24 Hicks, *Improper Pursuits*, 248, 323.

25 Hicks, *Improper Pursuits*, 284.

26 Quoted in Hicks, *Improper Pursuits*, 319.

27 From an autobiographical fragment published in Rosamund Brunel Gotch, *Maria, Lady Callcott: The Creator of "Little Arthur"* (London: John Murray, 1937), 64.

28 Donoghue, *Passions Between Women*, 147.

29 Quoted in Donoghue, *Passions Between Women*, 147.

30 Callcott, quoted in Gotch, *Maria, Lady Callcott*, 64.

31 The incident is described in a letter from Damer to Mary Berry quoted in Frances Borzello, *A World of Our Own: Women as Artists* (London: Thames and Hudson, 2000), 104.

CHAPTER SIX.
RATIONAL DAMES AND
LADIES ON HORSEBACK:
SCIENTISTS AND TRAVELERS

1 Maria Edgeworth, *Letters for Literary Ladies*, quoted in Margaret Alic, *Hypatia's Heritage: A History of Women in Science from Antiquity to the Late Nineteenth Century* (London: The Women's Press, 1986), 175.

2 Patricia Phillips, *The Scientific Lady: A Social History of Women's Scientific Interests 1520–1918* (New York: St. Martin's Press, 1990), 108.

3 Phillips, *The Scientific Lady*, 181.

4 Phillips, *The Scientific Lady*, 182.

5 Quoted in the *Dictionary of National Biography*.

6 Helen Ashton and Katharine Davies, *I Had a Sister: A Study of Mary Lamb, Dorothy Wordsworth, Caroline Herschel, Cassandra Austen* (London: Lovat Dickinson, 1937), 146.

7 *Dictionary of National Biography*, quoting from Caroline Herschel, *Memoir and Correspondence of Caroline Herschel*, ed. Mrs. John Herschel (London: John Murray, 1876).

8 Herschel, *Memoir and Correspondence*, 75–76.

9 Phillips, *The Scientific Lady*, 161.

10 Quoted from a letter from Miss Beckedorff, a friend of Caroline Herschel's, to Herschel's niece, December 1846, in Herschel, *Memoir and Correspondence*, 358.

11 "A Great Fondness for Botany," biographical essay in Larry J. Schaaf, *Sun Gardens: Victorian Photographs by Anna Atkins* (New York: Aperture, 1985), 23–40. Schaaf's essay gathers together most of what is known about Atkins's life, and the account here is largely dependent on his.

12 Schaaf, "A Great Fondness for Botany," 30.

13 As Carol Armstrong notes in *Scenes in a Library: Reading the Photograph in the Book, 1843–1875* (Cambridge, Mass.: MIT Press, 1998), 186.

14 Schaaf, "A Great Fondness for Botany," 32.

15 Schaaf, "A Great Fondness for Botany," 31. Schaaf points out that Atkins's failure to note where she collected each specimen "would have been a source of frustration for serious algologists" (32), although this seems, a bit unfairly, to exclude her from this group.

16 Schaaf, "A Great Fondness for Botany," 35.

17 Quoted in Alic, *Hypatia's Heritage*, 159.

18 Doris Langley Moore, *Ada, Countess of Lovelace: Byron's Legitimate Daughter* (London: John Murray, 1977), 316.

19 Moore, *Ada, Countess of Lovelace*, 231, quoting from a letter of April 4, 1835.

20 Mary Somerville, *Personal Recollections from Early Life to Old Age* (London: John Murray, 1873), quoted in Alic, *Hypatia's Heritage*, 157.

21 Alic, *Hypatia's Heritage*, 179–80.

22 Alic, *Hypatia's Heritage*, 159.

23 Moore, *Ada, Countess of Lovelace*, 45.

24 Alic, *Hypatia's Heritage*, 159.

25 Alic, *Hypatia's Heritage*, 172. Somerville is quoting from St. Paul, 1 Corinthians, 15:47, playing on Paul's words that "the first man is of the earth, earthy." (*Adamah* is "earth" in Hebrew.)

26 Letter to Babbage, July 2, 1843, quoted in Moore, *Ada, Countess of Lovelace*, 157.

27 See Moore, *Ada, Countess of Lovelace*, 243.

28 Charles Meryon, *Memoirs of the Lady Hester Stanhope, as Related by Herself in Conversations with Her Physician* (London: Henry Colburn, 1845), 2: 13.

29 *Memoirs of the Lady Hester Stanhope*, 2: 5.

30 Virginia Childs, *Lady Hester Stanhope: Queen of the Desert* (London: Weidenfeld and Nicolson, 1990), 179.

31 Pamela Neville-Sington, *Fanny Trollope: The Life and Adventures of a Clever Woman* (New York: Viking, 1997), 108.

32 Frances Trollope, *Domestic Manners of the Americans* [1832], ed. Pamela Neville-Sington (New York: Penguin, 1997), 18.

33 Trollope, *Domestic Manners*, 27.

34 Pamela Neville-Sington, Introduction, *Domestic Manners*, xiii.

35 Trollope, *Domestic Manners*, 72.

36 Trollope, *Domestic Manners*, 92.

37 This and the preceding quotation are from Trollope, *Domestic Manners*, 56.

38 Maria Graham, *Journal of a Residence in India* (Edinburgh: Archibald Constable, and London: Longman, Hurst, Rees, Orme and Brown, 1812), iii.

39 Lady Romilly, quoted in Elizabeth Mavor, comp. and ed., *The Captain's Wife: The South American Journals of Maria Graham 1821–23* (London: Weidenfeld and Nicolson, 1993), 6.

40 Jane Austen, *Persuasion* [1817], ed. John Davie (London: Oxford University Press, 1998), 159.

41 "Lady Callcott," obituary, *The Gentleman's Magazine*, January 1843, 99.

CHAPTER SEVEN.
THE YOUNGEST ROMANTICS

1 Letter of July 22, 1842, in *The Letters of Elizabeth Barrett Browning to Mary Russell Mitford*, ed. Meredith B. Raymond and Mary Rose Sullivan (Winfield, Kans.: Armstrong Browning Library of Baylor University; the Browning Institute; Wedgestone Press; and Wellesley College, 1983), 2: 7. I have changed the ampersands of the original to "and."

2 Margaret Forster, *Elizabeth Barrett Browning: A Biography* (London: Chatto & Windus, 1988), 317.

3 Both quoted in Margaret Reynolds, "Critical Introduction" to Elizabeth Barrett Browning, *Aurora Leigh* [1857] (Athens: Ohio University Press, 1992), 7.

4 Lyndall Gordon, *Charlotte Brontë: A Passionate Life* (London: Chatto & Windus, 1994), 8–9.

5 Gordon, *Charlotte Brontë: A Passionate Life*, 60.

6 Quoted in Juliet Barker, ed., *The Brontës: A Life in Letters* (New York: Viking, 1997), 11.

7 Gordon, *Charlotte Brontë*, 31.

8 This came about largely because of the title of Susan Gilbert and Sandra Gubar's now-classic work of feminist criticism, *The Madwoman in the Attic: The Woman Writer and the Nineteenth-century Literary Imagination* (New Haven: Yale University Press, 1979; 2nd ed., 2000).

9 Charlotte Brontë, *Jane Eyre* [1847] (New York: Random House, 1943), 80.

10 Brontë, *Jane Eyre*, 61.

11 Lyndall Gordon in *Charlotte Brontë: A Passionate Life*.

12 Charlotte Brontë to George Smith (her publisher), quoted in Barker, *The Brontës: A Life in Letters*, 368.

13 There is much discussion of the question in recent historiography of the eighteenth and early nineteenth centuries, but the locus classicus is Ruth Perry, "Colonizing the Breast: Sexuality and Maternity in Eighteenth-century England," *Journal of the History of Sexuality*, 2, no. 2 (October 1991): 204–34.

14 Quoted in Lynn Vallone, *Becoming Victoria* (New Haven: Yale University Press, 2001), 5.

15 Vallone, *Becoming Victoria*, 43.

16 Entry for September 24, 1852; quoted in Vallone, *Becoming Victoria*, 25.

17 Vallone, *Becoming Victoria*, 40–43.

18 George Eliot, *Selected Essays, Poems, and Other Writings* (London: Penguin Books, 1990), 333.

19 Quoted in Jennifer Uglow, *George Eliot* (London: Virago, 1987), 196, from Gordon S. Haight, ed., *The George Eliot Letters* (New Haven: Yale University Press, 1954–56, 1978), 5: 58.

SUGGESTED READING

The following highly selective list is intended only as a starting point for readers who want to explore further women's part in the history and culture of Romantic-era Britain. More titles can be found in the notes, and books cited there are not repeated here; and because biographies of specific individuals may be easily found in library catalogues, they too have been omitted.

Armstrong, Nancy. *Desire and Domestic Fiction: A Political History of the Novel.* New York: Oxford University Press, 1987.

Brewer, John. *The Pleasures of the Imagination: English Culture in the Eighteenth Century.* New York: Farrar, Straus and Giroux, 1997.

Clark, Anna. *The Struggle for the Breeches: Gender and the Making of the British Working Class.* Berkeley: University of California Press, 1995.

Colley, Linda. *Britons: Forging the Nation, 1707–1837.* New Haven: Yale University Press, 1992.

Davidoff, Leonore, and Catherine Hall. *Family Fortunes: Men and Women of the English Middle Class, 1780–1850.* Chicago: University of Chicago Press, 1987.

Donald, Diana. *The Age of Caricature: Satirical Prints in the Reign of George III.* New Haven: Yale University Press, 1996.

Fay, Elizabeth. *A Feminist Introduction to Romanticism.* Malden, Mass.: Blackwell, 1998.

Feldman, Paula. *British Women Poets of the Romantic Era.* Baltimore: Johns Hopkins University Press, 1997.

George, M. Dorothy. *Hogarth to Cruikshank: Social Change in Graphic Satire.* New York: Walker, 1967.

Jones, Vivien. *Women and Literature in Britain, 1700–1800.* Cambridge: Cambridge University Press, 2000.

Lynch, Deirdre, ed. *Janeites: Austen's Disciples and Devotees.* Princeton: Princeton University Press, 2000.

McCreery, Cindy. *The Satirical Gaze: Prints of Women in Late Eighteenth-century England.* Oxford: Clarendon Press, 2004.

Mellor, Anne K. *Romanticism and Gender.* London: Routledge, 1993.

Midgely, Clare. *Women Against Slavery: The British Campaigns, 1780–1830*. London: Routledge, 1992.

Prochaska, F. K. *Women and Philanthropy in Nineteenth-century England*. Oxford: Clarendon Press, 1980.

St. Clair, William. *The Reading Nation in the Romantic Period*. Cambridge: Cambridge University Press, 2004.

Trumbach, Randolph. *Sex and the Gender Revolution*. Volume One, *Heterosexuality and the Third Gender in Enlightenment London*. Chicago: University of Chicago Press, 1998.

Vickery, Amanda. *The Gentleman's Daughter: Women's Lives in Georgian England*. New Haven: Yale University Press, 1998.

ACKNOWLEDGMENTS

My greatest debt is to the co-curator of *Before Victoria*, the exhibition, Stephen Wagner, Curator of the Carl H. Pforzheimer Collection of Shelley and His Circle of The New York Public Library. While the writing and responsibility for errors are mine, his taste and choices are seen throughout this book, and his camaraderie and sardonic humor made hard labor easier. The generosity of Carl H. Pforzheimer III made both the exhibition and the book possible.

I should like to thank readers of drafts of *Before Victoria*, who saved me from mistakes and infelicities, and gave me what every writer needs, fresh points of view. Chief among these and indefatigable in her labors was Doucet Devin Fischer. She and Daniel Dibbern of *Shelley and his Circle* have been tolerant, patient, and kind throughout the writing process. Lyndall Gordon was a model of affability and generosity in her work on the Foreword. Jill Hammer, Nora Nachumi, Stephanie Oppenheim, Julie Shaffer, and Fiona Wilson were generous with both reading and friendship. I am especially grateful to the editors and designers at The New York Public Library's Publications and Graphics offices, Barbara Bergeron, Karen van Westering, Kara van Woerden, and above all Anne Skillion, who spent more time with this project than anyone besides its author.

In addition, Margaret Glover, Elizabeth Wyckoff, Nicole Simpson, and Ann Aspinwall of the Library's Miriam and Ira D. Wallach Division of Art, Prints and Photographs have been unstinting with their expertise. An anonymous reader for the Columbia University Press offered welcome encouragement. Frank Felsenstein gave a handy reference on Maria Edgeworth, and Michael Phillips a salutary lecture one night in the middle of an intersection of Broadway, and to them both, my thanks. Finally, for her love and support throughout, my deepest gratitude goes to Elaine Chapnik.

INDEX

Page numbers in *italics* refer to illustration captions.